THE IMPOSTOR PHENOMENON

Overcoming The Fear That Haunts Your Success

Dr. Pauline Rose Clance

Peachtree Publishers, Ltd.

Published by
PEACHTREE PUBLISHERS, LTD.
494 Armour Circle, N.E.
Atlanta, Georgia 30324

Manufactured in the United States of America

First printing

Library of Congress Catalog Number 85-60596

ISBN: 0-931948-77-0

Composed by Typo-Repro Service, Atlanta
Printed by Donnelley Printing Co., Harrisonburg, VA

To my parents, brothers, and sisters,
for providing me with love and challenge.
To Lanier and Nancy,
for encouraging me to be all I can be
and to take risks.

THE
IMPOSTOR
PHENOMENON

Table of Contents

Acknowledgments

THE TERM *Impostor Phenomenon* was coined and developed by me and Dr. Suzanne Imes, an Atlanta psychotherapist and long-term colleague, while we were doing research in 1974. We spent many hours discussing the experiences of our clients and students, and together we began to develop and write about the characteristics of these high-achieving people who doubted their abilities and competency. We worked together to develop effective treatment strategies for our clients and for use in our workshops.

Without Dr. Imes's excellent contributions to the original ideas, the present book would not be possible.

My warmest thanks to Emily Ellison for her excellent ideas, her editing and help on the present book.

Author's Note

TO PROTECT THE identities of those people who have contributed to my understanding of the Impostor Phenomenon by coming to me as clients, or who have participated in my research studies, I have changed ancillary information and combined cases when doing so would not violate the fundamental dynamics involved. The case histories do represent the real life struggles of people who suffer from the intense experiences of the Impostor Phenomenon. However, any similarities between these composites and any actual individual or family is purely coincidental.

Preface

ITS FRIDAY AFTERNOON. You have just arrived in
town to visit a friend, and although the two of you have
planned the entire weekend, your friend suggests you stop
by his office first. His company has just made a big sale,
and an impromptu party is being thrown. It's a good
chance for you to meet some of his co-workers, he says. So
you attend the party, standing around the crowded office
lobby with a drink in hand, listening to the shop talk of
others.

Through one of the office doors comes an attractive,
well-dressed woman. She carries a neatly arranged tray of
hors d'oeuvres, offers a taste to someone, places the tray on
a table, reaches out and shakes someone's hand, laughs, and
gives a friend a hug. You can hear her voice now. It is
articulate, and she is charming.

"Who is that?" you ask your friend.

"Oh, that's Margaret. She's the one who pulled off this
sale."

You say that she must be really sharp to handle such a
deal. "Oh, yeah. Margaret's great. She can do anything."
Later you're introduced, and you congratulate the woman
on her recent success.

She gives you a nervous laugh and says, "We were just
lucky this time."

"Don't listen to her," someone says. "She's being modest."

Margaret gives you a wink. "Don't listen to *him*," she
says. "He knows how much help I had." Someone touches

her on the shoulder, and Margaret excuses herself to begin a conversation with someone else. You hear mention that Margaret is the one who quickly prepared the food for the party, that Margaret has just received a promotion, that she handles more accounts than almost anyone else in the company. It appears your friend is right: Margaret can do anything.

But what neither you, nor your friend, nor probably anyone else at the party knows is that Margaret doubts she does anything very well. When she gave you the nervous laugh and shrugged off your congratulations, Margaret wasn't displaying false modesty; she truly believes she was lucky. She thinks the sale was made because she did have help, because she had worked hard, and because everyone does consider her sweet and charming.

What you probably also haven't realized is that Margaret is very introverted. Her sweep through the party is very difficult for her, and she's constantly on guard, trying to make sure she commits no faux pas, that she doesn't appear foolish, that she doesn't reveal how scared she is that she can't keep up the good work. And you probably never would have guessed how often Margaret compares herself to everyone else in the room, and that in her eyes she's never as quick or as clever or as creative as all the rest of you. You never would have guessed — Margaret is an "Impostor."

The IMPOSTOR PHENOMENON occurs with great frequency among successful, high-achieving people such as Margaret. They've done well in school, earned the correct degrees, received awards and praise from their colleagues, and advanced rapidly in their careers. In fact, in most minds, these people have it made. So the question usually arises, "If they've done so well, what is the problem?"

The answer is that their success is never truly fulfilling because, like Margaret, they're always too busy trying to make sure no one finds them out. Impostors believe they are intellectual frauds who have attained success because they were at the right place at the right time, knew someone in power, or simply were hard workers — never because they were talented or intelligent or deserved their positions.

Nearly all of us have known such people — the young female executive who secretly admits to close friends that the only reason she got the job was because "they needed a woman"; the male dental school student who over a few beers one night says the only reason he was admitted to dental school was because "my dad is a dentist"; the artist who believes his paintings were bought because a patron "felt sorry for me"; the counselor who is given a substantial raise and promotion, yet says only, "I worked my head off — they had no choice but to give it to me"; the actress who gets the lead role in a new play and then says to her husband, "I think the person they really wanted must have dropped out of the running."

In both my research and my work as a practicing psychotherapist, I constantly see men and women who have every reason to be on top of the world; instead they're miserable because in their eyes they never measure up. They believe they are never as bright or as talented or as sharp as others in their fields. They believe their success has come from every reason in the world except the real one: they had the ability and the brains.

When I was in college and graduate school, I experienced the symptoms myself. Even though I was doing well, I kept thinking that I might fail on the next examination. I was worried that I couldn't keep repeating my successes. I watched many of my friends experience the same feelings. We felt alone, however, and did not realize that our experience — the IMPOSTOR PHENOMENON — was very prevalent among other high-achieving people.

As a faculty member at Oberlin College and at Georgia State University, I met many students and members of the staff and faculty who had Impostor symptoms. In lectures and workshops on the subject, Dr. Suzanne Imes and I found that across the country people from many different professions experienced a haunting fear that they could not continue repeating their successes and that they were not as bright and as capable as they needed or wanted to be, even though there was strong objective evidence that they were truly intelligent.

Such fears and self-doubts make it almost impossible for these people to relax and feel comfortable with their success and with themselves. That's a frustrating way to live. And that's the reason this book was written.

Success doesn't necessarily mean happiness, but at the same time it shouldn't cause guilt, fear, and stress. And even when a mask fits well — even looks good on a person — there comes a time when that mask grows heavy, uncomfortable, and probably suffocating. Sooner or later, the mask needs to come off. That's what this book is all about — helping people to realize there are ways to remove the Impostor Mask and keep it off; helping people such as Margaret to know that they can be charming and gracious without feeling like fakes, that they can believe the compliments of others without feeling arrogant, that they can achieve great success without feeling guilty.

Hopefully, too, it will help people who suffer from the IMPOSTOR PHENOMENON to learn to accept their very special talents and intelligence and to learn to be comfortable with and proud of what these gifts may bring.

Dr. Pauline Rose Clance
Atlanta, Georgia

Putting On The Mask

1 | The Impostor Experience

MOST PEOPLE WHO experience the Impostor Phenomenon would not put such a label on themselves, nor would they overtly say, "I feel like an impostor." Yet when they hear or read about the components of the phenomenon, they immediately say, "How did you know exactly how I feel?"

And how do they feel? Someone once said that the ABC's of success are "ability, breaks, and courage." But most IP (Impostor Phenomenon) victims, even though they are often very successful, feel their success has been due to some mysterious fluke or luck or great effort; they believe their achievements are due only to "breaks and courage" and never the result of their own ability. They're also pretty certain that, unless they go to gargantuan lengths to do so, success can't be repeated again.

Following are examples of the kinds of people who have come to me in my practice, certainly not calling themselves "Impostors" but suffering from numerous fears, guilt, and an overall dissatisfaction with their lives. Those who admitted they were successful were unable to enjoy and appreciate that success. These individuals are representative of the many people hiding behind Impostor Masks.

THE IMPOSTOR PHENOMENON

BEVERLY

Beverly is an artist who has received local, regional, and national recognition for her work. Critics have given her good reviews, and her work has begun to sell. Yet if Beverly were asked if she's a successful artist, she would say no.

No, she doesn't think her work is as good or as original as it should be. And although a painting might be acclaimed, she always believes that it could have been better. She thinks of some way the color or texture could have been improved, and she feels certain that when people get her paintings home, they're going to realize they made an error or paid too much money for the work. Of course, when no one does return her paintings or demand their money back, she tells herself it's only because these patrons don't want to admit their foolish misjudgment.

When Beverly is scheduled to have an exhibit of her work at a local gallery, her doubts soar. She's certain the critics will laugh; she's afraid they will write something about her having the audacity to call herself an artist at all. She's fearful that people will have no idea what she's trying to convey and that they will realize how imperfect her work is. She's convinced she can't meet her deadlines, and she has thoughts of cancelling the show. Reassurances from her family and friends do not help; she has trouble eating and sleeping, and she becomes irritable and jumpy.

Beverly's assured by those who love her that she's always this way before a show, and yet the shows always go well. But she is only convinced that they don't understand and that this time it will be different: this time the show will be a certain failure, and she'll be humiliated and ruined.

On the evening of the show, attendance is excellent. The gallery is filled with other artists, art critics, and interested patrons. These people claim they are excited about her work and most give it great praise, but Beverly dismisses the compliments, thinking that her friends are only being nice. During the course of the evening, much of her work sells, and part of it will be used to decorate a high-rise office complex. It's harder for Beverly to dismiss the sales than it was to dismiss the praise, and slowly she begins to feel better. Later she receives two very complimentary reviews in the local newspapers. These articles are thorough and show a good understanding of her work. Finally she begins to think that possibly, after all, she really is a success.

But Beverly's newfound belief in her talent doesn't last long. A few weeks after the show is over and she's struggling to begin new work, her old doubts return. She knows she can't keep doing the same kinds of paintings, and yet she can't think of any new approaches. Why can't I be more creative? she asks. Why is this work so hard? Why do I have to struggle so much when other artists find it so easy? She begins to compare herself to all the other artists in town. After all, they seem to flourish while her creativity seems to be drying up. She's been working for weeks with very few new ideas, she repeatedly tells herself. Soon all the old fears come back to haunt her, and the success of the last show amounts to nothing.

JANE

A graduate student working towards her Ph.D. in sociology, Jane has always done excellent work and received mostly A's throughout her educational career. Recently she has been accepted to a graduate program in a good school and has received a teaching assistantship there. Letters of recommendation from the faculty at her college have been excellent, and her professors have voiced their beliefs that she will be an outstanding student.

Yet despite the accomplishments and praise, Jane experiences a great deal of doubt about her own intelligence and her ability to achieve. She senses that others may expect more of her than she can produce, and she's afraid they will discover she's not really as bright as she appears. Of course, in the past she has always been able to cover up all the details and information that she didn't know, but this time she fears she may not be able to continue that pattern.

Her first examination is scheduled. Even though she has never come close to failing such an exam, she's so worried and anxious about this one that she becomes nauseated and can't eat for several days before the test. Every spare moment is spent studying, and every night is filled with dreams about the exam. In these dreams, her professor passes out the examination papers while she sits frozen; she's unable to understand the questions and unable to produce a single answer. The dreams increase Jane's anxiety, and she becomes painfully aware of all the material she believes she has only skimmed and doesn't know thoroughly.

On the day of the exam, Jane gets up early and reviews all of her notes. She's still so nervous and unsure of herself that when she arrives at class, her hands are trembling. But when the examination is placed in front of her, she reads the first few questions and begins to relax. Her dreams haven't come true; she understands the questions and knows the answers. Jane writes furiously throughout the exam, relieved by all the details she remembers.

Afterwards, several of the other students in her class invite her to join them for beers at the local bar. Once everyone has arrived, they begin to discuss the exam and explain their interpretations and anwers. Jane believes all the other answers sound excellent, far superior to hers. Why hadn't she thought of such things? Why hadn't *she* answered that way? When the attention is turned to her, she says she's afraid that she failed. Everyone tries to console and encourage her, but now she's near tears. She tells her roommate later that she's certain she failed the exam and that she's going to start looking for a job.

A week later the test is handed back, and to her great surprise, Jane has received an A. Once again she has succeeded, and temporarily she feels great. But three weeks later another examination is scheduled, and once again she goes through the same painful process of great doubt and fear that she will fail. Once again she studies vehemently, and once again she enters the examination room certain that she's unprepared. But this time, too, she does well, receiving a B + when several students fail and none receives an A.

Jane's major professor tells her she's doing extremely fine work, but she doesn't believe him, and she's afraid she can't possibly keep performing well. Although she succeeds over and over again, she remains unconvinced that she really is a very intelligent, competent woman.

RALPH

Ralph is a successful lawyer with a good private practice — a general practice with considerably more variety than a specialized one. He often accepts difficult cases which other attorneys refuse to handle, and he takes on clients who are poor and may not be able to pay the going legal fees.

To Ralph, the most exciting part of his practice involves going to trial, and his trial success rate is very high. Because of this winning record, he often receives referrals from his colleagues and from his former clients.

He's grateful for these referrals, although he's a little surprised each time he receives a new one. Ralph knows he's a good trial lawyer, but he doubts his knowledge and abilities in other areas of the law. He's therefore afraid of making terrible mistakes that might interfere with the success of his case and cause grave consequences for his clients.

This fear of making a mistake results in his studying hour after hour at the law library, where he tries to delve into every possible ramification of a decision. His need to handle each case absolutely perfectly also leads to procrastination, and he usually finishes his work on a case at the latest possible time.

Ralph's tendency to procrastinate and his drive to develop perfect cases are all signs of his failure in his mind. Consequently, he dismisses all the times he has succeeded. In addition, when he compares himself to his father, who is a nationally known surgeon and faculty member at a major university, Ralph considers his accomplishments very minor and inconsequential.

SHERI

Like many other women, Sheri began her career as a secretary. But instead of staying in that position, she worked her way up in a local booking agency and even became an associate owner of the company. Because she enjoyed the work and felt she knew it well, she decided to try opening a similar business of her own.

She presently is doing so well that she has a staff of five and is netting more than $70,000 a year for herself. Yet when someone comments on her success or asks her to speak at seminars or businesswomen's panels, she quietly and firmly attributes her success to good luck or to her stamina and extremely hard work.

Sheri seems afraid to acknowledge even to herself that she has excellent judgment and that she has made very good business decisions in the past. She believes that much of her success has been due to an uncle, who helped her find her first job and who is well known in the area for his business cunning and brilliant ventures.

She also has the omnipresent notion that she could not repeat her success. Since she attributes her achievements and position in the business world to good luck, hard work, and knowing the right person (her uncle), she's driven by the fear that she can't continue with as much success. When she is approached to open a similar business in another city, she turns down the opportunity, positive that she couldn't make it go.

JENNIFER

The only black nurse in a managerial position at a large federal agency, Jennifer has mixed emotions about her success. On the one hand, she feels very pleased about her position, but at the same time she continues to be amazed that she's doing so well. She is very much liked and respected by her colleagues, she has received excellent evaluations, and she continues to receive honors and special recognitions and awards.

But one evening she confides to a close, trusted friend that she obtained her present position because the agency needed to employ women and minorities to meet federal hiring requirements. "And I was a black woman," she explains to her friend. "That's the reason I am where I am."

In her explanation of why she was hired, Jennifer totally ignores her own credentials — her excellent academic background and her former job experiences.

When she talks to her family, Jennifer also downplays the importance of her position at the agency. She never lets them know about the awards and excellent evaluations she has received, and when she is chosen as one of the most prominent, successful young women in her city by a well-known magazine, she doesn't send them a copy of the article. To do so might make her seem proud and arrogant, she feels. She also has the superstitious belief that somehow she may become a loser if she dares to boast about her success.

HAROLD

Harold has an uncanny ability to remember facts, analyze data, review literature, write excellent reports. Before entering college he scored very high on the SAT, and he always does exceptionally well on any standardized exam. Yet Harold doesn't consider himself to be *"really* intelligent."

He discounts his writing talent, his test scores, and his tremendous ability to remember facts by saying, "Those aren't signs of intelligence. Those things come easily for me."

At the same time he dismisses his true talents, he also dwells on all the things that are hard for him to do and labels them examples of "real intelligence." For instance, Harold's brother writes poetry and is very original. He's considered the intelligent, creative one in the family. Harold therefore believes the kind of writing *he* does — grant proposals and reports — is very dry and unoriginal compared to his brother's poetry. Because of this, he also considers himself not very bright or successful.

In truth, the more "creative" brother rarely writes poetry and mostly works at odd jobs. And even though Harold is the one who is successfully employed, who is sought after as a consultant on grant proposals, he continues to believe his brother is certainly more capable than he.

~ ~ ~

All of the people previously mentioned come from different economic and social backgrounds. They're all in different fields, at different levels of their careers, and they all have different talents and abilities. Yet there is one thing common to Beverly, Jane, Ralph, Sheri, Jennifer, and Harold: they are all intensely experiencing the Impostor Phenomenon. They've all received objective, external evidence that they're bright, successful, talented people, yet they doubt that objective evidence and question the reality of their success or their intelligence.

These six people are all afraid they are impostors — that somehow they've tricked others into believing they're more capable and knowledgeable than they really are. None of them is convinced of his or her innate talent and intelligence. And they're all concerned that the next time they have to prove themselves or repeat their past performances, they will fail.

Yet at the same time, these Impostors work very hard to prove themselves wrong. They want very much to succeed and to believe in their success. They're continually striving for excellence and recognition and to show others that they are capable.

THE IMPOSTOR PHENOMENON

These Impostor feelings are generally well-kept secrets. And the people who have them believe they are very much alone — that their situations are unique — and certainly that no one else shares the sense of shame and discomfort they do.

When these people learn that they indeed are not alone, that many others experience the Impostor Phenomenon, there's usually a great sense of relief. They're pleased to learn that what they've experienced secretly is a wide-spread feeling among highly successful people. They're usually pleased too when they learn that what they've been living with has been discovered and researched and that it has been given a name.

In reading the earlier descriptions of the six people, you may have recognized IP traits or actions that are characteristic of you or someone you know. If so, you'll probably be interested in taking the IMPOSTOR TEST.

7. I tend to remember the incidents in which I have not done my best more than those times I have done my best.

    1   2   3   4   5

8. I rarely do a project or task as well as I'd like to do it.

    1   2   3   4   5

9. Sometimes I feel or believe that my success in my life or in my job has been the result of some kind of error.

    1   2   3   4   5

10. It's hard for me to accept compliments or praise about my intelligence or accomplishments.

    1   2   3   4   5

11. At times, I feel my success has been due to some kind of luck.

    1   2   3   4   5

12. I'm disappointed at times in my present accomplishments and think I should have accomplished much more.

    1   2   3   4   5

13. Sometimes I'm afraid others will discover how much knowledge or ability I really lack.

    1   2   3   4   5

14. I'm often afraid that I may fail at a new assignment or undertaking even though I generally do

well at what I attempt.

1   2   3   4   5

15. When I've succeeded at something and received recognition for my accomplishments, I have doubts that I can keep repeating that success.

1   2   3   4   5

16. If I receive a great deal of praise and recognition for something I've accomplished, I tend to discount the importance of what I have done.

1   2   3   4   5

17. I often compare my ability to those around me and think they may be more intelligent than I am.

1   2   3   4   5

18. I often worry about not succeeding with a project or on an examination, even though others around me have considerable confidence that I will do well.

1   2   3   4   5

19. If I'm going to receive a promotion or gain recognition of some kind, I hesitate to tell others until it is an accomplished fact.

1   2   3   4   5

20. I feel bad and discouraged if I'm not "the best" or at least "very special" in situations that involve achievement.

1   2   3   4   5

~ ~ ~

After taking the Impostor Test, add together the numbers of your response to each statement. If your total score is 40 or less, you have few Impostor characteristics; if you scored between 41 and 60, you have moderate IP experiences; a score of betwen 61 and 80 means you frequently have Impostor feelings; and a score higher than 80 means you often have intense IP experiences. The higher the score, the more frequently and seriously the Impostor Phenomenon interferes in a person's life.

If you scored in the moderate to high range on the test, remember that you are not alone. Many successful people have similar scores.

It's also important to know that having intense IP feelings does not mean a person has a pathological disease that is inherently self-damaging or self-destructive. It probably does mean, though, that the Impostor Phenomenon is interfering with that person's ability to accept his or her own abilities and to enjoy success. And it probably means that there's an unusual amount of doubt and anxiety in that person's life. As a result of these feelings, IP sufferers often limit their goals and stay in positions that are below their true capabilities.

These people are generally tired of having so many doubts and worries, and they want to gain a realistic view of their talents and their achievements. Mainly, they want finally to be able to enjoy their successes — they want to enjoy life.

In the following chapters, we'll be identifying the different components of the Impostor Phenomenon. We'll learn how IP feelings originate and why. And, most importantly, we'll learn ways to cope with and overcome Impostor feelings.

3

The Impostor Profile: An Overview

E VEN AFTER READING the previous chapters, you may still wonder exactly what type of person is most vulnerable to the Impostor Phenomenon. First of all, we're talking about people who have received objective, verifiable evidence that they are capable, competent, and successful in their areas of endeavors. The objective criteria may be good grades or high IQ scores, good performance evaluations, the ability to get and to hold good jobs, or being able to flourish in a profession or career.

Do not confuse Impostors with others who may fail in one or more of those areas or people who fake their credentials, pretend to have received good objective praise, are fradulent in their performances, or who know they're bright and successful but shrug off compliments in an act of false modesty.

We're talking about people who have valid, tangible accomplishments yet are haunted by the fear that they cannot keep repeating their successes, or that they are somehow not as capable or as bright as they appear to others. These people are painfully aware of any deficiencies that exist in their knowledge. They tend to see others' strengths and abilities and to admire and overrate the intelligence or achievements of those around them, always comparing themselves to these people, always believing that in such comparisons they come up short.

THE IMPOSTOR PROFILE

Not every person with IP feelings will have all of the following characteristics, but they will have at least two or three. Those who scored high on the Impostor Test are likely to have more of the traits than those with lower scores. As you read, try to select the parts of the profile which most fit you or someone you know who is dealing with Impostor feelings.

1. THE IMPOSTOR CYCLE

Persons with IP feelings experience considerable self-doubt and worry excessively. They're frightened that they cannot repeat their accomplishments. They remember all their difficult times more than their successes or the tasks they previously completed with ease. They dwell on all the things they do not know rather than thinking about all the knowledge they've gained. They're constantly worried that they may not be able to live up to others' expectations of them. The question, "How good am I really?" is generally in the backs of their minds.

When faced with a need to perform, they experience doubt, worry, anxiety, and fear; they're so afraid they won't be able to do well that they procrastinate and sometimes feel they're unable to move at all toward completing the task. In other cases, they overwork and overprepare and begin much sooner than needed on a project, thus robbing themselves of time and effort that could be better spent. Those who have procrastinated finally begin working with a sense of panic, trying frantically to get the work accomplished on time. When the project is completed and they receive acknowledgments about its success, they are temporarily relieved and happy. But the next time a similar situation arises, the whole vicious cycle is repeated, and the success of the previous project is negated. IP victims soon develop the superstitious belief that they must endure all of the torment again in order to succeed, thus making the Impostor Cycle a very difficult one to break.

2. THE NEED TO BE SPECIAL, TO BE THE VERY BEST

Often IP sufferers have been the top performer, or at least among the very best, in their childhood or adolescent years. When they reach college or obtain an important position in their fields, they soon realize they are only one among many exceptional people. They have great difficulty accepting the reality that they cannot remain No. 1 forever. They yearn to be special and often secretly wish to be a genius. Too often they dismiss their real talents and presume they are stupid if they are not the very best.

3. SUPERWOMAN/SUPERMAN ASPECTS

Due to their need to be the best, Impostors are very perfectionistic in almost every aspect of their performances. They expect to do everything flawlessly and with ease. Being human, of course, makes this goal difficult or impossible to obtain, and these people generally feel overwhelmed and that they have failed.

4. FEAR OF FAILURE

These people experience terror when they think of failing at some goal they have set for themselves. They experience extreme anxiety when they think they've made a mistake; they take drastic measures not to err or to appear foolish in front of others. Because shame and humiliation are equated with making mistakes or not performing at peak level, they work very hard to make certain they never fail.

5. DENIAL OF COMPETENCE AND DISCOUNTING PRAISE

IP sufferers are ingenious in their ability to deny or disclaim the objective evidence that they are indeed intelligent and/or successful. They refuse to accept and internalize any obvious proof that they are competent, and they cleverly develop ways to discount such proof. They distort any resulting praise and are unable to accept positive feedback.

6. FEAR OF AND GUILT ABOUT SUCCESS

Some people with IP feelings have a real fear of success. Women are especially likely to have this symptom. Although they want to be very successful, they are frightened of the consequences of that success. For many women, there is a concern that a high level of success may interfere in their relationships with men and that they will be seen as threatening or unfeminine.

Men may have a fear of success because they have received messages that they must not be more successful than their fathers. Some men have also received signals from their families or through their religious upbringing that they should not be competitive.

People who perceive their success as atypical of their family, race, sex, or the region in which they live may experience guilt about that success. Concerns about separation and rejection play a large role in their utilizing Impostor feelings so they can say, "I'm not really different. I'm not really more successful than everyone else." Thus, their Impostor feelings provide them with a way to remain humble.

Impostors also are afraid of success because they're fearful of being asked to take on even more responsibilities. If they were to acknowledge their success, rather than having Impostor feelings, they think that incredible demands would be made of them — demands they might not be able to meet.

~ ~ ~

IP victims usually make excellent first impressions, and they are able to put up a good front and effectively disguise their imagined deficiencies and weaknesses. Unfortunately, this ability to appear one way while feeling quite another adds to the feeling of being an Impostor and to an overall dissatisfaction with themselves.

In fact, Impostors suffer a great deal. They tend to be introverted rather than extroverted (although on the surface it might appear that the opposite is true), and they question themselves regularly. They rarely experience the joy and satisfaction and sense of accomplishment that can come with success, and they are not able to truly let themselves feel confident about their ability to continue succeeding. Their symptoms can lead to unnatural levels of misery, anxiety, and depression. At times the victims feel helpless and hopeless and think, "No matter what I do, it's not enough. I never can be really successful." They feel ashamed of their doubts and usually keep these feelings secret.

Is change possible? Can IP victims learn to get real pleasure from their successes and come to believe that they are truly competent and intelligent? The answer is definitely yes. I have seen many victims change and become relaxed, confident individuals.

Of course, a key element to change is the recognition that one is a victim. As I've said before, people with IP symptoms do not go around saying, "I feel like an impostor." They do not label their feelings as IP feelings, but rather as objective truths about themselves. Therefore, becoming aware of and recognizing one's symptoms are critical steps in overcoming the phenomenon.

Specific strategies also are effective in overcoming IP sensations. As the person practices regularly these coping mechanisms, which will be discussed in detail later in this book, they can begin to experience positive change.

Other IP victims may find that they are unable to deal with their symptoms alone and may want to obtain professional help from a qualified psychotherapist or counselor, who can help them identify more clearly the Impostor patterns in their lives. In my experience, psychotherapy is very effective in helping to bring about change for such people. After therapy, many clients are able to state truthfully and joyfully, "I no longer feel like an Impostor. I'm able to savor my success and accept my intellectual abilities."

But, as I said earlier, before change can take place, a

person has to decide if he or she is an IP victim. Therefore, let's start by taking a look at the well-intentioned Mask Makers and how the Impostor Phenomenon begins.

4

Those Well-Intentioned Mask Makers

IF YOU WERE to examine the surface of a typical Impostor Mask, it more than likely would have a nice confident smile, a look of authority around the eyes, and a certain self-assuredness in the face. But if you were able to touch the Impostor Mask, like all masks it would feel artificial, unreal.

If you were able to go a step further, to put a finger under the top of the mask and begin to lower it, you would find that the face hiding underneath is actually nothing like the synthetic one on top. The two faces may resemble each other in color of eyes, facial structure, complexion, and shape of lips, but the face underneath would be far from confident, and there certainly would be no look of authority or self-assurance there. If anything, the face would look anxious, scared, and tired. There may even be a bit of panic to the face, as if it were beginning to suffocate under the heavy mask.

Your first response probably would be to pull the mask back up quickly, because even though you know it's a false face, it's better than looking at that distressed one you saw underneath. But then after the mask was safely back in place, you probably would become curious, and your second response would be to ask why the person was wearing a mask in the first place. How did it get there? And who made such a mask?

To truly understand the Impostor Phenomenon and those people who experience it with such intensity, it's essential to start at the beginning — with the Impostor's family.

Most of us have clear views of ourselves. We see ourselves as "tall," "friendly," "insecure," "creative," "selfish," "bossy," "stocky," or "caring." Whatever tag we put on ourselves, no matter what it is, that tag tends to stay with us most of our lives. But why did Sally first begin to think of herself as a "selfish" person? And why does Jack, no matter how thin he becomes, think of himself as "stocky"? And why does Karen, no matter how agreeable she is, always think of herself as "bossy"?

Chances are that most of these people first heard these same descriptions of themselves when they were very young. Many of our fundamental views about ourselves — and eventually our views about our own competence and our potential for success — began with our families and how our parents and/or siblings saw us and how they conveyed what they saw. These messages given to us when we are very young, stay with us and have a profound effect on the self-image we develop.

Parents want to transmit their fundamental values and views of the world to their children, and they begin by instructing their children in how they want them to act and how they want them to be. The family soon assigns attributes to each child, and by the stories that are told and the messages that are given, the child begins to take on the characteristics that the family has described.

In looking at the origins of the Impostor Phenomenon,

four common elements of the families of its victims stand out:

1. THE FAMILY'S IMAGE IS NOT THE WORLD'S IMAGE

There often is a discrepancy between the feedback a child receives from his or her family and the feedback he or she receives from teachers, friends, neighbors, or other relatives. When this happens, the child doesn't know which messages to believe — the ones being received at home, or the ones that come from everyone else. Since the child's very survival in the world is dependent upon his or her family, the child is torn by the inconsistent images that apparently are being seen.

2. FIRST COMMANDMENT: BE SMART

The second common element of IP families is that they place very high importance on the child's being able to learn quickly and to maneuver well in the world. Often stories are told about aunts, uncles, cousins, or friends and whether or not these people have been bright enough to get ahead and "make something" of themselves. From a very early age, the child understands that it is valuable to be "smart," and that if he is going to make it in the world, he needs to be a fast learner.

3. THE FAMILY'S SQUARE PEG

The third common element is that the child perceives his or her abilities and talents to be atypical of the rest of the family's. For example, a child may be a mathematical genius while the other members of the family care nothing about numbers but tend to have artistic or musical talents. The child begins to feel that he or she is "different" and even begins to feel like the proverbial square peg trying to fit in the family's round hole.

4. A LACK OF PRAISE

The IP family does not openly acknowledge a child's abilities or celebrate and reward accomplishments. There are usually many different reasons for this lack of praise. Sometimes it comes from well-meaning parents who are afraid that too much applause may make a child arrogant. Others fear it may make the child appear too different from other children. Some parents may simply have chosen another sibling to be the "star" or bright one in the family, and they don't want to admit their mistake. And some are so certain that their children are outstanding that they expect them to be "the best" and don't acknowledge each individual accomplishment; instead they take their children's successes for granted. Some parents may brag to friends and relatives about what their offspring have done, but they rarely let these children know how proud they are of their achievements.

These overt discrepancies and sometimes covert messages can create the feelings of being an Impostor in a child. How these elements are carried out in a family vary considerably. The following case studies were developed to show how three very different families affected the development of three very bright people.

ELEANOR

Very few women had ever received an advanced degree in nuclear engineering from the university where Eleanor went to graduate school. The fact that Eleanor did earn such a degree and is working in a field traditionally dominated by men, makes her exceptional.

Yet, as is characteristic of people with IP feelings, Eleanor dismisses any evidence of her success and her ability. She believes the only reason she was admitted to graduate school was that one of her college professors had gone there and had used his influence. This same professor had once told Eleanor that she looked and acted like his wife, and she therefore believes this is the reason he pushed her as an applicant. What Eleanor fails to realize is that he could not have gotten her into such an excellent program if she had not had the qualifications and the intelligence to do well there.

This woman's family background is illuminating. As a child she was always expected to do extremely well on anything she attempted. Her parents always had the attitude, "Of course Eleanor will do well at school," and it was assumed that she would learn with ease. They conveyed the notion that they expected and wanted her to achieve, to be special, to rank among the very best. When she did bring home excellent grades or outstanding scores, they barely seemed to notice because, of course, she was doing what was expected.

Eleanor also developed the idea that she should never make mistakes or admit failures. Because she had adopted her parents' standards and believed that she should do well in everything, she became miserable if some subject matter was difficult for her to grasp; if it was hard for her, then she must be stupid, she decided. At school, when she began to realize that some students were just as intelligent as she was and that occasionally some might even be brighter, she became afraid that others (especially her parents) might find out: they might discover that she wasn't so smart after all. So rather than show her possible stupidity, she became quiet and rarely spoke up in class. Her reticence only made matters worse; she became self-critical about her silence, believing that if she truly was bright, she wouldn't be afraid to answer questions or offer her opinions at school. Because of this silence and the lack of interaction, she was never able to learn what people thought of her ideas, and because she was afraid to ask questions, she actually began to have some real gaps in her knowledge which caused her to be quieter still in an attempt to hide what she didn't know.

In addition to expecting her to be very intelligent and accomplished, her parents were extremely noncritical. They never told her that she had made a mistake or error, and they never pointed out any of her faults. Consequently, she didn't trust their judgment. Since they obviously couldn't see her mistakes or faults, they couldn't be realistic judges of her ability; therefore they must be overestimating her potential, she believed.

Yet she was afraid they might discover their error in judgment and realize that she wasn't nearly as capable as they thought. She hid her doubt and anxiety, though, and began to avoid any competitive situation where she might not win. For example, Eleanor was a poor speller, so on the day a spelling bee was to be held, she pretended to be sick in order to prevent her parents from knowing she wasn't the best in her class.

Her parents' high expectations of excellence contributed to Eleanor's developing severe Impostor feelings. She experienced great pressure to be outstanding, to be special, to be the very best. And because she generally achieved these things, she was accepted at the best schools and into the best programs, where she was surrounded by other people who were also "outstanding," "special," and "the very best." In the midst of these other superlatives, she began to think, "I'm not very bright at all. I don't really belong here."

And just as her parents did not voice any criticism during her formative years, they also did not fully acknowledge what Eleanor actually accomplished. Since they expected so much, they were nonchalant and somewhat indifferent when she obtained her advanced degrees and began succeeding in a field that traditionally employed very few women. They didn't recognize the effort, the talent, the ability, and the difficulty that came with what she had achieved. They often talked to relatives and friends about all she had done, but they rarely told Eleanor how important or wonderful they thought it was.

The discrepancy in the feedback that she received from her parents (that she could do *everything* well) and that which she received from teachers and friends (that she did extremely well in some, but *not all*, things); the importance of intellectual pursuits and accomplishments that were stressed in her family; her success in scientific subjects, which was atypical of a family which normally succeeded in artistic endeavors and the social sciences; and the lack of open praise for her accomplishments all contributed to Eleanor's development of IP symptoms in grade school. These characteristics followed her throughout high school and college. And even now that she has received her degree in nuclear engineering and obtained a coveted position in her field, these Impostor feelings remain.

THE IMPOSTOR PHENOMENON

RALPH

The successful attorney whose experiences were discussed in Chapter One had a very different family background. Ralph's father was a devoted physician whose knowledge of medicine and the practice of medicine were the most important aspects of his life. He spent very little time with his son, and when they were together, he tended to be critical of Ralph, saying such things as, "No, that's not the right way to do that. Let me show you how."

If Ralph brought home a report card filled mostly with A's and an occasional B, the father ignored the A's and focused on the lower grade, asking, "What went wrong in History? What happened here?" And when Ralph wanted to show his father something new he had learned, such as a new equation in chemistry, his dad replied, "That's nice, but have you also learned the latest theory about nuclear fission?" If Ralph had an idea for a new project, his father immediately asked questions such as, "Have you thought of the cost?" "Do you think your method of construction will hold up?" "Don't you think it would be better to . . ." "Have you considered . . ." By the time his father had gone through his list of suggestions, Ralph felt stupid and unable to think. He began to feel that he never would be able to really please his father. Gradually he began internalizing his father's perfectionistic and critical standards, and he became hypercritical of himself.

He could perform a task extremely well, but if it were theoretically possible to do it better, Ralph felt that he had failed. He also began to expect others to treat him the same way his father always had. In college, one of his teachers wrote on a paper Ralph had prepared, "Excellent work — perhaps we can edit it for publication." Instead of being proud of this remark, Ralph experienced a great deal of pressure. He feared the professor would find a hundred things wrong with the paper if it was scrutinized in the editing process and, in working with Ralph, would discover all that he didn't know. He avoided the professor and never tried to get the paper published.

After Ralph was out of law school and established in a practice, he was always surprised when he received praise from colleagues and clients. He was unable to accept and believe their praise; instead, he began thinking there was something wrong with the people who didn't criticize him. If he accepted their opinions, it meant his father was wrong. And since he couldn't tolerate the thought of his father having been too strict or too perfectionistic, he negated other people's praise instead.

There was one other thing covertly tied in with Ralph's negative feelings about himself. If he actually admitted his own success, he might also have to admit that he could compete with his father. And yet Ralph thought there was no way he could ever finish better than second in that competition. His attitude therefore became: Why try?

In Ralph's family system, the high demands placed on him, coupled with the strong critical responses of his father, led to intense Impostor feelings. In addition, his father had achieved great success and recognition, and Ralph felt that he could never match that success. His mother had always stayed out of the interactions between him and his father except occasionally to say, "Your father loves you and doesn't mean to hurt your feelings." Ralph indicated only that his mother's opinions didn't count much in their family and that his father was the one with the power, brains, and money.

Ralph had received scholarships and excellent evaluations from outside authorities; this was very different from the feedback he got from his father. His family valued intelligence, yet the study of medicine was what really counted; his success in working with people and in learning law was atypical for his family. It was rare that he received any recognition or praise for the things he did well. Ralph's family history definitely had all the elements that contribute to Impostor feelings.

JANE

Jane, the young student described in Chapter One who had a fear of examinations and worries over her success in graduate school, grew up in a family with five brothers and sisters. Each child in her family was distinguished by a particular characteristic that the other members had labeled him or her with. For instance, Nadine was "the troublemaker" and was expected to have problems. Mary was "the helpful one," who was loved by everyone. Irene was considered "the competent, intelligent one." David was "the math whiz." Paul was known as "the likable one." Last was Jane — the baby — "the lazy, spoiled one."

She grew up believing the family myths about her brothers and sisters and accepted the idea that each was like the description that had been assigned. This meant that she also believed the description of herself being the lazy, spoiled child.

Jane learned to read quickly and it became one of her true loves. Early on her teachers began to show an interest in her and often complimented and encouraged her. Whenever a visitor came to class, Jane was nearly always the one called upon to read aloud. It was only natural that when she went home, Jane wanted to show off how much she had learned and how well she read, but no one seemed very interested in this aspect of Jane.

It was always Irene, "the competent, intelligent one," whom Jane's parents considered bright. The traditional family stories always included ones about how quickly Irene learned to walk and to speak and how she quickly and easily found solutions to problems. So when Jane began receiving good grades and praise from her teachers, she thought that she too might be as bright as Irene.

But when she shared her news about some accomplishment or showed her good grades, her family was unimpressed. Jane's own doubts began to emerge, and she began to think that perhaps the family was right and she wasn't as smart as Irene. Her parents and siblings also conveyed the notion that they believed Jane played up to the teachers, and that was why she received mostly A's.

In spite of the lack of encouragement, Jane finished high school with honors, graduating with the third highest grade point average in a class of more than two hundred. She also won speech contests and was acclaimed for her ability to move and inspire an audience. She impressed many teachers and evaluators, but she couldn't impress her family. They still thought of her as "lazy" and treated her like the "spoiled" baby of the family.

They also dismissed Jane's teachers and professors as having no common sense and being "stuck up." It was implied that "book-learning is not all there is to life." Jane's mother often told her stories about people who had become highly educated and who had thus lost their sense of humility and their friendliness. And when Jane studied particularly hard, her family reminded her of a boy from the mountains who had gone off to medical school and studied so much that he eventually went crazy. Jane knew this boy was a grown man who wandered around in a cowboy outfit, indeed appearing insane and talking nonsense. When she thought about this man or listened to the family stories, she became frightened that if she studied hard she would go crazy too, or, at very least, lose her sense of humility. Yet Jane knew she had to study hard to do well — after all, she wasn't the bright one in the family, just lazy and spoiled. She desperately wanted to disprove both family myths, but both haunted her.

There is another important aspect to Jane's case history. Her academic success was atypical for her family. No one else in her family had received a college education. Even Irene, the one who was considered so intelligent, had dropped out of school and married at an early age. Jane therefore often felt guilty about her success and didn't want to seem proud or arrogant to her family. One way to remain humble, and remain accepted by the other family members, was to have strong Impostor feelings.

~ ~ ~

Although the three family histories mentioned here are quite different, they all have the four critical elements which help to create the Impostor Phenomenon. Eleanor, Ralph, and Jane all received both covert and overt messages that (1) it was important to be smart; (2) their talents and achievements were atypical of their parents' and siblings' talents and achievements; (3) their families saw them differently from the way the world saw them; and (4) because of the lack of any open and real praise, they believed their families thought their accomplishments were very unimportant or unimpressive.

Generally, families develop these patterns out of the

parents' own childhood experiences and reactions to them. And most often, families give children the messages that they think will teach them how to live successfully in the world. For instance, the critical father may think that if he's not demanding and stern, his child will become lazy and irresponsible. The mother who warns her daughter about the pitfalls of higher education may truly believe that if these stories aren't told, her daughter may grow up to become a person who has no common sense.

What is really important is that Impostors be able to remember what their family messages were. When they understand the messages, they can decide if the messages were incorrect and need to be changed. It's also important for people who have IP feelings to know that the impact of what parents or siblings said or implied can be changed without rejecting the love or the care that came from these family members. Following is an exercise to help Impostors remember the messages that were sent by parents and siblings and help them discover if the characteristics they were tagged with are correct.

~ ~ ~

Get yourself in a relaxed position and apply the following questions to yourself or to someone you know who may have IP feelings.

Who was the favorite child in your family?

Who was the most intelligent one in your family?

How did your family decide who was the brightest?

THE IMPOSTOR PHENOMENON

Who made the best grades in school?

Who has the most education?

How did your father define intelligence?

How did your mother define intelligence?

What was your family's attitude toward bright people?

What stories did your family tell you about yourself as a youngster?

Did these stories convey to you what attributes your parents thought were important?

Which teacher from grade school do you remember most?

What did he/she think of you?

Which teacher from all of your education do you remember most?

How did the teacher's opinions compare with your family's opinions?

How were your major abilities or talents different from or similar to those of your parents and/or siblings?

After answering these questions, try to remember how

you handled any discrepancy between the feedback you received from your family and that which you received from others, such as teachers or neighbors. If there were such discrepancies, did they cause you to have doubts?

If you presently have occasional doubts about your ability, can you remember when these doubts began to emerge? Did you ever share such doubts with your family or teachers, and if so, what was the reaction? Often IP victims have confessed their self-doubt only to feel that their concerns were not heard or weren't taken seriously, causing them to grow more and more secretive about how they truly think of themselves.

Did you in any way disappoint your parents by following a career that was atypical for your family or different from what they wanted or expected you to do? For example, did you choose to become a minister rather than the engineer your father always said you would be? If so, you may have discovered the source of some of your doubts.

How did your family overtly and covertly acknowledge your success? Were your parents among those who seemed to take for granted a child's accomplishments, or were they afraid too much praise might spoil?

As you look at these questions, you may find that you have from one to four of the elements that contribute to the creation of an Impostor Mask. If you do, knowing how your IP feelings and behaviors originated is likely to be helpful.

In the following chapters, we'll discuss many other ways to help Impostors to understand why they act as they do and to help them cope with and overcome their fears and insecurities. But first, before we deal with how to remove the Impostor Mask, let's take a closer look at the person underneath.

The Personality Behind The Mask

5 | The Impostor Cycle

A S WE DISCUSSED in Chapter Three, IP victims usually develop a pattern or cycle which they believe is essential to their success. As much as they would like to break this vicious cycle, to finally be free of the worry and anxiety that always comes with taking on a new task, they feel that such a break would insure certain failure. The sad thing about the Impostor Cycle is that it prevents successful people from ever really knowing success; it is a bit like being on a treadmill, where no matter how fast you go or how long you've been running, you never seem to reach your goal.

Marie is one of those persons who keeps going round and round, who can't — no matter how hard she works — free herself from the Impostor Cycle. Let's take a look at her and see if we can determine why.

MARIE

A high level administrator of a health program for the state, Marie has been invited to give an address at a national conference in her area of expertise. At first, she's pleased with the honor and prestige that are implied by such an invitation. But as the date for the speech draws nearer, she has a terrible dream. In this dream, while Marie is in the process of giving her speech, she keeps losing her place and forgetting what she wants to say. She cannot seem to remember a single word of the speech.

Days later the dream is still with Marie, and she begins to fear the real speech and wishes she could cancel it. She has fantasies in which no one shows up to hear her and others where the audience walks out when she starts to talk. She becomes anxious and agitated and has trouble actually working on the speech. She procrastinates preparing for it until the very week before the conference, and then she sits up four nights in a row, working hour after hour.

When she arrives at the convention, she's terrified that her speech will be a tremendous flop and that her colleagues will learn how little she really knows. She's absolutely certain that if she gets through the speech, she won't be able to answer questions well.

To Marie's surprise, a huge audience shows up. At first she's nervous, but she begins to calm down as she gives the speech and sees the interest of the audience. She speaks fluently and spontaneously; all questions are answered with skill. At the end of her talk, she is given a standing ovation. Marie has succeeded again.

For a short time, she feels that maybe she actually is a success and not a failure after all. Temporarily her Impostor feelings subside, but the next time she faces a challenge, the doubt, worry, and anxiety return — and with as much force as they did before. In fact, she begins to deny the reality of the previous accomplishment and certainly negates the degree of the success.

Ironically, as in Marie's case, success actually reinforces the need for the Impostor Cycle. In fact, if we look closely at the cycle, it becomes obvious that the anxiety, fear, and worry are reinforced more than the ensuing success. The sequence of behaviors practiced by Marie are as follows:

> Invitation — Acceptance — Joy/Good Feelings — Bad Dreams/Worry/Fear — Immobility/Procrastination — Frenzied Work — Success — Praise — Relief — New Challenge — Denial of Previous Success — Fear Again.

With Marie, as with others running on the seemingly endless tracks of the Impostor Cycle, the ovation, praise, and relief followed her path of worry, self-doubt, fear, and hard work. She therefore feels that the only way to achieve such success again is to follow this same pattern. She maintains the superstitious belief that if she doesn't experience worry, doubt, anxiety, fear, and other Impostor feelings, then she also can't succeed.

She pays a high price for her achievements, but she thinks it's a price she has to pay. In fact, Marie can't imagine being successful in any other way. She never even dreams that accomplishments can come without all the pain.

WHY CHANGE?

Since this cycle often does result in actual success, the question may arise, "So, what's the problem? If it works so well, why would anyone want to change?"

The problem with the Impostor Cycle is that the feelings of anxiety, self-doubt, and dread increase the amount of stress involved with success and decrease the sense of satisfaction that should come with it. And as a result of this stress, IP victims may have nightmares or suffer from insomnia. Many even have physical symptoms such as headaches, stomachaches, eye twitches, or other similar ailments. After the cycle is completed, many also experience disappointment, dread, and depression. Consequently, it's very important that these people learn to break the cycle and know that they can succeed without all the unnecessary stress.

Many people who have the Impostor Phenomenon try very hard to undo their doubts, yet they usually discount their abilities by saying that they succeed only because they work harder, longer than anyone else. After all, they theorize, if they had to work so hard to accomplish something, then they must not be very bright. Truly intelligent people accomplish everything with ease, they believe.

The other problem with the hard work aspect of this cycle is that many IP victims work harder than is necessary to do something really well. George Bernard Shaw once said, "When I was a young man I observed that nine out of ten things I did were failures. I didn't want to be a failure, so I did ten times more work." Impostors feel much the same way, working many times harder than necessary, even when they haven't failed in the past. For instance, a student may study many more hours than is needed to make an A on an exam; or an attorney may spend twice the time necessary to adequately prepare a good brief; or a commercial artist may spend an entire day completing a display for a store window when an hour or so would have been sufficient.

These people who overwork to achieve usually recognize that their behavior is self-defeating and unnecessary, but they are afraid to change this behavior due to their fear of failure and their fear that others may discover their imagined inadequacies. At times, these people are so anxious and overworked that they aren't as effective or as efficient as they normally would be spending far less time on a project. As hard as they work, their doubt interferes with their functioning at peak level.

The Impostor Cycle is one of the most important elements of the phenomenon; until the cycle is broken, it's difficult for IP victims to function normally and be at ease with their success. To understand the cycle better, it's helpful to know when it's most likely to occur.

IMPOSTOR PRIME TIME: THE FIRST JOB

People who are beginning their careers or just entering the job market are likely to experience IP feelings at a very intense and often painful level. As these people begin looking for employment, they tend to say to themselves, "I've received all this education and training, but I don't know if I can make it in the real world. Although I made good grades and obtained good evaluations, the real test is how well I do now."

These people feel intense pressure to prove themselves, and they want desperately to know that they will be successful. Many of the IP characteristics listed in Chapter Three emerge, and the Impostor Cycle is likely to begin when they start their first jobs.

The following case study is a good example of someone who is beginning a career and facing that critical Impostor Prime Time.

JIM

I first met this young man while he was still in medical school specializing in internal medicine. Jim was an articulate and likable person — tall, slender, and good looking. He was also shy and didn't realize how attractive he was. He entered therapy in order to deal with a certain amount of depression he was experiencing and his fear of relationships with women.

He continued his therapy work during his internship and his residency, and he was eventually able to recognize that people did indeed like him. He also became much more confident about how physically attractive he was and less guilty about his sexuality.

But one day after he had finished his residency work, I noticed that he turned pale when we began discussing his plans of opening his own practice. I quietly told him that he looked frightened, and I suggested he close his eyes, take a deep breath, and see what emerged. After a long silence, he tearfully explained why he had looked so distraught. "I'm very afraid," he said. "I'm so afraid that I can't make it in the real world."

"Stay with your fears," I said, "and see if you can determine what you're afraid of."

"I'm afraid I don't know how to do it. I'm a good doctor, I know, but I hate all the business aspects. I don't know a thing about how to set up an office. And I hate having to go to banks and trying to sell myself."

"OK, you're pretty confident that you're a good doctor," I said, "but you're at the point where you need to do all kinds of things that are new and scary to you, like getting loans, and you're afraid you can't do that. You're also having to do things that you detest having to do."

"Right. I don't like dealing with the world," Jim admitted. "I always feel I can't do it well. I feel shaky and uncomfortable, and I hate having to put up a good front to try and impress people."

I tried to assure Jim that all the details he feared taking care of were things he had had no experience with, and it wasn't surprising that he should be scared. "Those things are difficult," I said.

"Then you think it's OK that I'm scared?"

I again assured him that I did, and I told him that I thought beginnings are always hard. Then I asked him if he had considered getting some expert help with the business aspects of establishing a medical practice.

The question startled him, but at the same time he also looked pleased. After a few moments he said, "You mean you'd think it was all right to hire some help — not to do it all alone?"

I told him I certainly did. "In fact, I'd recommend that you do just that, and I can give you the names of two or three excellent people." He seemed troubled at that remark and I asked him what was wrong.

"Somehow I think I should do it all myself."

"How come?"

"Because if I don't do it alone, then it won't really be my success."

"Where did you get that notion?" I asked.

"I was just taught that I should be able to do everything well. I should be able to handle it all myself."

"You probably could handle it all yourself," I told him. "But I think you'd be much less frightened if you had some help, if you got away from the idea that you must do it alone. Can you remember who taught you that?"

"My mother thought I was special and brilliant and that I could do anything I wanted to do."

"So if you could do anything you wanted to do, then you should be able to set up this practice alone, and you certainly shouldn't be frightened."

"Right."

"But you are frightened."

He nodded. "Yes."

"And you may need help."

Very hesitantly he again said, "Yes."

Finally, after more discussion, Jim was able to realize he didn't have to do it all alone and that it was all right for him to ask for assistance. He hired a consultant who helped him make the best business decisions and freed him to do what he chose to do — practice medicine.

In Jim's case we can see how facing the start of a career brought about an overwhelming amount of fear and worry and caused him ultimately to feel almost paralyzed in making a decision or making a move on setting up his practice. It's also obvious that he was dealing with a need to be special and a fear of not being able to do everything perfectly. As he came closer to starting his own private practice, his fear of success also emerged.

During a later session he made the following comment: "I'm afraid I won't make it on the one hand, and I'm afraid I'll make it too big on the other."

"Tell me more what you mean," I said.

"Well, if I fail and don't get enough patients, I'll feel awful. I've put eleven years into becoming a doctor, and I will have wasted all that time if I can't do it. Yet if I really make it the way I see other doctors doing, I may not have any time to enjoy my life."

"If you fail, it'll be awful. You'll feel terrible. And you don't think you can stand failing."

"No, I don't."

"Have you *ever* failed at something you've put real energy and work into?" I asked.

"No. I haven't."

"How real is it that you may fail this time?"

"Well, I have met a few internists who didn't make it in practice, but most do."

"So what is real for you?"

"I probably can make it. A lot of people have said they'd like a doctor like me, but it's going a lot slower than I expected."

"You wanted to have a full practice right away. You thought you were supposed to succeed immediately, is that it?"

"Yes, that's right. And if I don't, then I think I'm a total failure."

"What do you really think is the truth here?" I asked.

He hesitated a moment, then said, "I'm slowly succeeding. Patients are beginning to come to me and they're giving me good, positive feedback."

I then asked Jim to repeat what he had just said and try to internalize it. "Try to believe it."

"Patients are coming and they are liking me," he said. "They'll probably come back and send other people." This time he was relieved and seemed to believe what he was saying.

"What about the fear that you'll succeed too much? Tell me more about that."

"My practice will get so full that I'll have to work sixty, eighty hours a week, and I'll have no time to myself. I don't want to work all the time. I've seen too many physicians who never have any family life."

"You want to play as well as work."

"Yes. I want to have children and be able to really father them."

"If you're too successful, you won't be able to do that."

"Right."

"Is it possible to limit your practice? To stop taking new patients after a point?"

"Yes, theoretically. But most doctors don't."

"You're afraid you can't say no."

"Yes, that's very hard for me. I want to be liked."

After this session, we spent considerable time on his developing the intention to succeed in a way that suited his wants. He began to realize that he didn't have to duplicate the model of success that most doctors had presented to him. But as his practice grows, he will need to continue to learn ways to say no. He also will have to utilize, over and over, the strategies outlined in Part Three in removing the Impostor Mask and breaking the Impostor Cycle.

IMPOSTOR PRIME TIME II:
NEW PROJECTS, NEW JOBS

Just as Impostor symptoms emerge in an acute way when IP victims are beginning their careers or starting their first jobs, they also surface when it's necessary to tackle a new project or when Impostors receive a promotion or take on a new position. At these critical times, people are especially concerned about making a good impression and wanting to be liked and respected by their employers and co-workers. Because of these concerns, IP victims have a tendency to say to themselves, "I have to prove myself all over again. I have to show these new people that I'm as good as I appeared to be during my interview or when they were considering me for a promotion. But I'm worried I can't live up to the picture I conveyed. In order to make a good impression, I emphasized my strengths and acted as if I knew exactly what I was doing. Now I'm wondering if I can really accomplish all I said."

Such IP victims were able to emphasize their strengths during interviews or important meetings with the boss, yet their doubts come forward when they're faced with the day to day work required by the new project they've taken on or in their new jobs. These people are correct in believing one thing — it's true that others tend to have high expectations of new employees. And it's true that people generally are hired or promoted or gain admission to a college or university because others were impressed with their abilities and potential for continued success. But these expectations, instead of encouraging, trigger the doubts of IP victims.

In Part Three, we'll examine ways to help alleviate some of this distress. But for now, to help explain why such situations create a prime time for the emergence of such intense Impostor fears, let's take a look at Mildred.

MILDRED

Mildred is a businesswoman in her early thirties who had advanced fairly rapidly in her company when she came to see me. She sought professional help because she was very tense most of the time and frequently ill. As we talked, she complained a great deal about her work and how unhappy and bored she was with it. She said that she knew the ins and outs of her business even though she had not been in her present position very long, and she wanted a job with more power and authority which would allow her to influence company policy.

She had a good relationship with a superior who carried a great deal of clout and prestige within the firm. I encouraged Mildred to let this man know about her aspirations and to ask him what chances he thought she had of being promoted. Although she was very hesitant to approach him on the matter, she did so.

In a few months she was promoted to a new position and became director of an important company program. But very soon after this promotion, Impostor fears emerged.

As we talked, she exclaimed, "I'm so anxious because I don't have any real clear direction to go in. I don't know how to proceed."

"You're very scared and confused. You don't know where you're going."

"Yes, and that's why I'm constantly anxious," she said.

"Why do you think you got this promotion?"

"Because I know a great deal about the needs in this area. I've handled all the grants and special programs."

"So you do know a lot," I stated.

"Yes," she replied quietly.

"Yet you're supposed to have a clearer direction for the total program now, even though you've had this position only one month. It seems to me you're expecting an awful lot of yourself."

"It does?" She seemed surprised.

"Yes. You're demanding that you be able to do it perfectly immediately."

"That's right. I really need to do it well. But there's so much I don't know."

"You're really frightened that you may fail at this."

"Yes, I am," she said. "My heart pounds, my hands get sweaty, and I can't sleep for worrying about it."

"It's very important that you succeed, and you're so afraid that you won't." I paused a moment and then asked, "What's the worst thing that could happen to you if you don't succeed?"

"They'd think I'm terrible and inadequate and

incompetent."

"And then what would happen?"

"They'd fire me."

"And then what would happen?"

"I'd be devastated. I'd feel so terrible that I don't think I could stand it. I'd be humiliated."

"I want you to know that I truly hear how scared you are and how anxious," I told Mildred. Then I asked if she knew where all the fear was coming from.

There was a long silence, and then she said, "My mom is like that. She always worries that she'll lose her job."

"Did she ever lose a job?" I asked.

"No. Never. She's worked at the same place for years. But when I talked to her about my promotion, she acted worried. She seemed to think that I've taken on more than I can handle."

"So she's afraid you may fail."

"Yes, she worries about me."

"And she's subtly giving you the message that you may not be able to handle all of this success."

"Right! I hadn't realized that."

"In contrast to your mom, what kind of feedback have you received from your boss?"

"He seems pleased," Mildred said. "He says I'm doing fine and that I have plenty of time to make decisions about the direction of my program."

"What if you believed him instead of your mom?"

Mildred laughed. "I'd feel a lot better."

I asked her to take a moment and try to internalize her boss's message that she was doing fine. She breathed deeply and concentrated. "Now, please close your eyes and fantasize yourself being more relaxed and confident. Visualize yourself being less anxious and more able to cope."

After I urged Mildred to do this, she began to relax some and said, "I don't have to do everything in one day. I'm doing fine. I do have good ideas to offer."

Many other sessions were spent on her need to be perfect, on her need to be the very best, and her tendency to overwork. With almost constant practice, she became less anxious and more able to enjoy her new success. Yet if she obtains another promotion, the same kind of practice may have to be started all over again. Like so many Impostors, each time Mildred has to prove herself anew, she finds that it's a prime time for all her IP feelings to emerge.

The Impostor Cycle, and the unnatural kind of frenzied, excessive hard work that comes with it, especially when IP victims are faced with new jobs or beginning their careers, usually comes from their ever-present fear of failure and their need to be special.

6 | Fear Of Failure

MOST INTELLIGENT PEOPLE know that almost everyone — no matter how successful or smart — occasionally has failed at some endeavor. We all know that a Pulitzer Prize in drama doesn't mean that same author's next play will be a smash. We know that even the best tennis players in the world occasionally go through dry spells, when they can't seem to win a single match. We've heard of the brilliant surgeon, who, in spite of his skill, will have a patient die on the operating table. We've heard the stories of Thomas Edison, who as a child had problems in his school work, even though he was later recognized for his genius in working with electricity. We know that Freud's ideas were rejected as absurd before his brilliance was recognized. We know that Van Gogh and his paintings were laughed at during his lifetime. We're aware of such things and know they're examples of what it is to be human.

Impostors are aware of such things, too. But Impostors are unable to apply this knowledge to themselves. Even though they know intellectually that failure is a necessary part of living, they can't tolerate the thought of it, and they avoid it at all costs.

They're afraid they would experience shame, self-hatred, and a total loss of self-esteem if they failed in their own eyes or in any way appeared less than capable to others. And they're afraid they couldn't possibly live through such humiliation. Their hard work, perfectionism, avoidance of difficult intellectual endeavors, and their push to excel and be special are all means of preventing any kind of failure.

CAROL ANN

This IP victim was a speech consultant for businesses and corporations. She was very successful in planning seminars, developing workshops, and giving demonstrations to firms at the local, regional, and national levels. Despite some previous Impostor fears, she was beginning to feel good about her abilities, and she decided to apply to be a workshop leader at a national convention for speech and drama teachers and consultants.

She submitted an outline for such a workshop to the program committee and quickly was accepted. But to her dismay, when she held her workshop, the other speech consultants treated her ideas with indifference. Rather than taking her format seriously and listening attentively to what she had to say, they swapped stories, told jokes, and didn't seem in the least impressed with Carol Ann.

Afterwards she felt shame and humiliation. She agonized over every interaction, played back every part of her leadership role. No one had been impressed with her methods, and she was certain she would never get another proposal accepted again. She was afraid she was being laughed at and might even be ostracized by others in her field. By all of her criteria, she had completely failed.

That evening, when she was having dinner alone, mourning over her failure, a man who had attended the workshop asked to join her. As he took a seat beside her, he began complimenting her on the job she had done and asked if she knew how many famous consultants had heard her. She said that, yes, she did, and that was one of the reasons she was so embarrassed by what a failure the workshop had been. Surprisingly, instead of being sympathetic, the man laughed. "Don't you know those people never seem to take these conventions seriously? Your only mistake is that you expected them to react like your clients."

At first she didn't know whether to believe him or not. Yet when she saw many of the participants later in the week, they were friendly and certainly didn't shun her. In fact, many were so wrapped up in themselves, she learned, that they didn't even realize she was the one who had conducted the workshop. She also learned, through later discussions with other colleagues, that most of these people were extremely competitive and rarely praised each other's work or ideas.

Carol Ann was one of those Impostors who had always been terrified of failing. And yet, this experience proved to be very important to her and added to her growth. She had failed in her efforts to be considered special by this group, but she had learned not to overemphasize the importance of such a failure. She learned that sometimes others are too preoccupied with their own appearances and successes to notice anyone else's, and the opinions of such people shouldn't really influence how she judged herself.

MERRY PAT

This college professor experienced a different kind of

failure. All of Merry Pat's credentials were excellent. Like so many other IP victims, she had received outstanding grades and evaluations all through school, had won many honors at the graduate and undergraduate levels, and had earned a Ph.D. from one of the country's most prestigious universities. Yet despite this glowing record, her contract was not renewed at the college where she had been teaching for the past two years.

The main reason the administration gave for the non-renewal was that she was not the kind of role model they wanted for their students. Merry Pat had been very active with the young people who were debating the issues of student participation in campus affairs.

Although she had always succeeded in the past, this dismissal was a devastating blow and created a tremendous amount of anxiety and pain. Many of her colleagues wanted her to sue the college, but she didn't think she could handle the additional stress and humiliation, especially if she were to lose the case. Instead, she obtained a research job with a major funding organization and received several promotions almost immediately. Pretty soon she was advanced to the position of director, where she was in charge of a huge budget and had tremendous influence over what kinds of scholarly activities received grants.

With her new success, she gained a new kind of confidence in herself. She also realized that had her teaching contract been renewed, she likely would have stayed in the same position indefinitely and would not have recognized so many of the other abilities she had. With this recognition, she began to lose her dread of failure and many of her Impostor feelings.

Although many Impostors, like Carol Ann and Merry

Pat, live in constant dread of failure, most of them, because they are human, do eventually fail at something. They lose an election, are fired from a job, or make an overt error that can't be hidden from others. When this happens, most IP victims are surprised to learn that they do survive the experience, and most actually prosper from it.

THE NEED TO BE SPECIAL

Some Impostors' fear of failure is so acute that they not only have to be good, they have to be the best. They have to feel that in some way they are very special.

We've all heard the old adage, "It's lonely at the top." Well, most Impostors who have this need to be special would give anything if only this were true. Unfortunately, to the shock and dismay of many of these people, they find that actually the opposite is the case. Pamela is a perfect example of the overachiever who learns that often there's quite a crowd at the top.

She came to me complaining of a number of anxieties and fears — nothing life threatening or terribly severe, but symptoms that were present often enough and intensely enough to interfere with the everyday enjoyment of her life. As she listed her feelings, it didn't take long to realize that Pamela was suffering from the Impostor Phenomenon. One of the strongest of her characteristics — like so many other IP victims — was her need to be the very best at everything she did, her need to be outstanding and special.

She was a successful journalist who had obtained a good job with a prestigious publication immediately out of college. She had been promoted quickly and moved around the country as one editor after another offered her an even better job. When she came to see me, she was not only making a good salary and receiving the choicest assignments, but constantly receiving praise from her employers and peers. But for Pamela, this was never enough. In her mind, each story she wrote always could have been better. And if, by the end of each year, she had not won at least one journalism award, she felt like a complete failure. She also felt threatened by the new talent always being hired around her, and she couldn't stand the thought of no longer being the youngest, the best, and the brightest in her profession. On the surface, it looked as if Pamela truly had the world by its tail: she made lots of money, she had worked for some of the finest publications in the country, her résumé looked like a list from *Who's Who in America*, she was considerd one of the best young writers in the country, and she was succeeding at the one thing she had always wanted to do. But underneath, Pamela was far from happy. The secret to her unhappiness was that she was considered "one of the best," not "*the* best."

Most Impostors who suffer from this need to be special were considered intellectually astute or different when they were growing up. Usually they had received special attention from their teachers and were told that they were particularly gifted; and most had received more than the normal amount of praise for their talents. They were the ones called on to perform, the ones everyone else considered the best.

Because of this preeminent beginning, they began to expect themselves to remain the most outstanding. For them, it could no longer be enough simply to be very bright or very competent and capable. From childhood on, they felt they had to be at the *very* top, to remain the "star." Therefore, when they later attended the finest colleges and universities, where there were many bright and outstanding people, they began to experience extreme Impostor doubts about themselves. They began to think, "I'm not so bright after all. I'm not so competent. I've just been fooling everyone all this time." It's almost impossible for them to realize instead that, yes, they're bright and capable, but so are many other people. They can't seem to say to themselves, "All of us can exist together, and I don't always have to be the most outstanding anymore."

The roots of this problem generally reach back to childhood, when these people did not feel accepted for who they were or what they experienced. Somehow, they felt that in order to be loved, they had to live up to their parents' expectations of their being the very best and learning everything with ease.

In Pamela's case, she not only compared herself to those she worked with every day, but to journalists throughout the country. She wasn't simply satisfied to be the best wherever she worked, but she had to be the best young journalist anywhere. And because this was an almost impossible goal, she negated her efforts and tended to see herself as a failure.

Gradually, as she worked with her Impostor doubts, she began to realize the futility of such goals and the waste of negating her very real accomplishments. Finally she understood how unrealistic it is for any one person to be the very best at any one thing — that in a competitive world such as ours, there are many superlative people in every field, but that doesn't mean a person can't be proud of the things he or she has accomplished and appreciate and enjoy the times they have been the one at the very top.

With time, Pamela came to accept her fine qualities and admit her success; and with time, for her, those things became enough.

STAYING AWAY FROM THE DIFFICULT

Some people with Impostor doubts — again, usually because they want to appear to be the brightest or the most special — tend to discontinue an activity if it's difficult for them or if there's someone present who obviously is better suited to succeeding at the task. Their need to be the best prevents them from trying anything they're not absolutely sure they can be outstanding at.

This need to be special also causes some IP victims to remain the "Big Fish in the Little Pond," instead of branching out and trying their luck at some of those larger ponds, where the competition is much more keen.

PAUL

When he was young, Paul was the kind of child who was fascinated by taking his toys apart and, to everyone's surprise, being able to safely put them back together again. During his adolescent years he progressed to the family's household appliances, finding as much pleasure with them as he earlier had had with his toys, tinkering with them, dismantling them, until he discovered how they worked. By the time he reached high school, he had moved to automobiles, and he was the one who could always be found under the hood of a friend's car, doing the work that only experienced mechanics usually knew how to do.

It was obvious he had a real aptitude for doing anything mechanical, and everyone began saying, "Paul can fix anything." But while he enjoyed this kind of work and could spend hours repairing a broken washing machine or rebuilding the carburetor on an old car, his secret ambition was to become a mechanical engineer.

His parents had always indicated that he could do anything he wanted to do and, because most things had always come easily to him and he never had to spend much time studying, he believed them. But when he began taking the math courses that were required to get into college, he experienced his first real obstacle. It was difficult for him to understand many of the mathematical concepts, and he had to study hard and struggle to learn what was expected. Yet, at the same time, he realized there were other students who zipped through the assignments with no problems and seemingly without any study or preparation. He immediately felt inadequate when he compared himself with these individuals.

When he talked with his teacher, she encouraged him to keep studying and to keep taking math courses. The guidance counselor at his school also indicated that his aptitude in math was good and that he did have the abilities that would be needed to do well as an engineer.

Paul, however, was not so sure. Even though he sincerely wanted to become an engineer, he was afraid he wouldn't be the very best. If there were students who were already smarter than he was in math, then obviously there would be engineers who were smarter and better too. Also, the process of taking the necessary courses and getting through college suddenly seemed too difficult.

He finished his math course and actually made an A, but he soon dropped his plan to go to engineering school. At an unconscious level, he decided not to tackle a task that would be hard and require real effort but to stick with the kind of work he had always done with ease. In his mind, he could not tolerate the anxiety that he felt when a subject was difficult for him to grasp.

After high school, then, instead of going to college, Paul

enrolled in a nearby technical school and became the No. 1 student in his class. He aced the program, gathered the necessary capital, and opened his own automobile repair shop. His business is prospering and financially he's doing well, but he's often sad and restless and fantasizes what his life would be like if he had studied to be an engineer.

Paul had the aptitude to get through college and become the engineer he had always dreamed of being. It would have required a good deal of studying and he probably wouldn't have been the very best student in all of his classes, but he could have accomplished his goal. Instead, he was so afraid of risking failure and so afraid of not being No. 1 in a temporary situation that he ended up with a job situation that, for him, was permanently second best.

NOT REACHING FOR THE TOP RUNGS OF THE LADDER

For others, the fear of failure is so great that they underestimate their talent and intelligence, and they aim for goals that are far below their capabilities. They work under the assumption that there's less chance of falling if they don't reach too high.

Norma is a prime example of such a person. When I first met her, she had no idea she could achieve what she later did accomplish, and she was headed toward a career that would have been unfulfilling and far from what she was capable of doing. Always interested in medical issues and health related work, Norma majored in biology with the hope of doing laboratory work in a good hospital setting. After college, she was hired as a lab technician, where she was able to get a close look at physicians and nurses working in all the different specialized areas of medicine.

Over a period of time she became friends with several physicians and learned that their interests were very similar to hers. However, despite the friendships, she kept these people placed high on pedestals, believing they must be extraordinarily intelligent to have succeeded as physicians. Susan, a good friend and one of the medical specialists, recognized Norma's interest and suggested that she apply for medical school. At first Norma was intimidated by the idea, having never before even considered the possibility. Finally, at the urging of friends, she went for a battery of tests administered by a clinical psychologist. These tests indicated that she definitely had the intellectual ability to do very well in medical school, and the psychologist encouraged her in this direction.

But even after receiving the test results, Norma was skeptical. Her doubts about her intellect — especially when compared to the physicians around her — persisted. It was only with great dread and self-doubt that she finally applied. She was turned down on her first admission effort, but her medical friends assured her this was normal and kept encouraging her to try again. She started taking some pre-med courses, and in the third year of admission trials, she was accepted by a fine medical college.

During her first year, she was continually terrified that she wouldn't make it. She studied long, hard hours trying to overcome her anxiousness and to assure herself of success. She finally began to realize that she was doing as well as all her classmates, and gradually she relaxed. Fortunately for Norma, others recognized her intelligence even when she did not, and because of their continued encouragement, she reached for goals that she never would have attempted by herself.

Many IP victims are not so lucky and stay forever in

situations that are far beneath them. It's sad that their tremendous fear of failure limits their degree of success and, at times, (because they are committed to staying at the bottom) even results in a very personal kind of failure.

"I CAN'T APPEAR FOOLISH!"

In addition to the other types of dread-of-failure we've already discussed, there's one more symptom that many Impostors possess. For them, there is an acute fear of appearing foolish or stupid. They do not give themselves permission to acknowledge that at times everyone, no matter how brilliant or capable, appears ridiculous or may feel like a fool in front of others. It's very likely that at some point in their early childhoods, they experienced shame or were humiliated by a parent, an older sibling, or a classmate. It's possible that they were teased for some mistake they made or for admitting something they didn't know.

It's also possible that they witnessed one of their parents, or another loved adult, looking foolish or dumb, and they experienced the adult's shame. At that time, they resolved never to have such feelings again or allow themselves to be part of a similar situation. And as adults, the thought of being humiliated or deeply embarrassed is still overwhelming; therefore, their goal is to never look stupid.

The problem with this goal — besides being unrealistic — is that people cannot avoid the possibility of appearing foolish without also squelching their spontaneity and creativity. When that occurs, IP victims recognize that they have killed an important part of themselves and feel more like failures than ever.

KATIE

The summer following her junior year of college, Katie worked as an intern at a small newspaper in a medium-sized Southern town. During that summer she was greatly encouraged by the city editor and told that she had real talent. When she left to go back to school at the end of her internship, he also promised her a job immediately after graduation.

Unfortunately, by the time she finished school and went to work, this editor had moved on to a new job and was replaced by a man who was not fond of Katie. He had been there the previous summer, working as a reporter, and had been jealous of all the attention she had received. Therefore, with his newfound power, he made sure Katie was given the worst assignments and worked only on the most uninteresting beats. Not wanting to lose her job or appear like a spoiled prima donna, Katie did not complain and worked at stories that were far less important than the ones she had covered as a college intern.

She stayed under this man's thumb until, a year and a half later, a male reporter, straight from college with no previous journalism experience, was hired and assigned to a major story. This was a story Katie had been working toward getting for months. When she complained to her city editor, he said the new reporter needed the experience and assigned her to write a far less important article. The months of acquiescing, of trying to do a good job while maintaining a hidden resentment, were suddenly too much. There was a huge, loud argument in the middle of the newsroom between Katie and the editor, which ended with her resigning and walking out.

It didn't take long for her to get another job at a larger

paper in a neighboring state. Katie worked very hard at this job, too, was promoted quickly and assigned to a very important, interesting beat. Yet despite her new success, the humiliation of the previous job and the fight with her boss haunted her. The last scene in the newsroom stayed with her for years; she was sure she had appeared like a fool in front of her colleagues, and she was painfully embarrassed that she had lost control. Because her humiliation was so great, she never returned to her former place of employment, although she had made many friends at the paper and had very much liked the town where she had lived. She also avoided running into any of these people when she attended professional journalism conferences, and she lived with the fear that the story of her first job would get to the people with whom she presently worked.

In truth, most of the people who had been present the day she quit had respected her stand and never thought of her as appearing foolish. But Katie's fear of such a situation was so intense, and her pain over it was so acute, she was never able to talk about it with these people and learn their true feelings. The result was that she lived with an unnecessary skeleton in her closet, which always clouded any new success. And because she was scared of such an incident occurring again, it was difficult for her to ever relax in her job and really be herself.

Since it's probable that most of us will experience some kind of failure and some disappointment as we work toward our goals, it's very important that IP victims learn how to cope with their fears of failure and learn to risk looking foolish sometimes. As they do, they will be taking important steps in mastering their IP feelings and eventually taking off the Impostor Mask.

7 | The Superwoman Aspect And The Perfectionistic Male

YOU'VE PROBABLY SEEN THAT commercial on TV where the blonde appears on the screen vampishly claiming she can "bring home the bacon, fry it up in a pan, and never, never let you forget you're a man." As trite as this ad campaign may be, there are many Impostors who could sing a similar song. For them, it's simply not enough to have a brilliant, successful career. They also must be able to perform in every area of their lives, and they must perform perfectly.

Two previous Impostor characteristics we've discussed — the tendency to overwork and the need to be special — are both tied to the pursuit of perfection. Not all perfectionists have the Impostor Phenomenon, of course, but many people with IP doubts do strive to be perfect.

Such individuals want all their work or ideas to be brilliant, creative, and productive *all of the time*. These people can't distinguish between which projects require the most intellectual output and excellence, and those which require only minimal effort and quality. For them, it is necessary to be perfect at everything they do; for them, it's necessary to become super human beings.

To better understand this aspect of the Impostor

Phenomenon, let's take a look at a woman we'll refer to as Susan.

SUSAN

As director of the physical therapy department in a large, university-connected hospital, Susan is responsible for administering the program, developing new ideas and establishing ongoing research, planning the budget, overseeing the quality of patient care, creating inservice training and staff development ideas, and making sure that her department is fairly treated within the hospital system. Such demands would be a load for almost anyone, but Susan's problems were multiplied by the fact that when she was appointed director, the department was in particularly bad shape. The quality of care provided patients was far from excellent, and the budget was nowhere near being met.

Nonetheless, Susan was able to advance the department's position in the hospital system and to improve tremendously the quality of patient care — all in less than a year. Naturally she received excellent feedback and evaluations because of these improvements, but her achievements did not satisfy her own standards of excellence, and she experienced strong doubts about herself as the director in spite of all the objective praise.

She also was unable to get a perspective on which areas of her work could receive modest attention versus those areas that required her very best efforts. She had difficulty in setting priorities, too, and in being able to say no to any request that was made of her. As a result, she spent an incredible amount of time after regular working hours trying to get everything accomplished and trying not to be overwhelmed by her position.

Susan was unable to trust her ability and not demand perfection in every aspect of her performance. For instance, she spent an unnecessary amount of time editing and rewriting certain memorandums that could have been sent as they were to the appropriate people or committees.

A considerable number of hours was also spent preparing for every staff meeting. It would have been possible for her to have developed one or two items for each meeting and waited for other significant issues to emerge as she and her staff talked. But because she wanted a perfect agenda, and because her lack of trust in her own intuitive and intellectual abilities spread to her notions about her staff, she was afraid no good ideas would come from the meeting without a tremendous amount of preparation on her part.

For Susan ever to be able to relax in her present position and appreciate the fine work she has done, she'll have to begin work on her Impostor doubts. She'll also need to become less perfectionistic on everyday projects and learn to hand in work that did not previously meet her standards of excellence. And she eventually will need to learn that only the most important projects require so much of her time and energy. If she learns these things, her chances of success probably will be greater than ever. Certainly her enjoyment of it will.

MOTHERHOOD AND IP FEELINGS

Many books have been written addressing the joys and problems of motherhood, and there is a need for much more research on these powerful and complex matters. But in this section I will be dealing only with mothering issues that are related to the Impostor experience.

Becoming a mother is a very special time when intense Impostor feelings are apt to emerge. For the first-time mother, trying to be a good parent can be a truly terrifying task. The stakes are higher than at any time the woman has ever known. This isn't simply a new challenge she's facing, she's dealing with a human life. Because of this, her hopes for her child are enormous and she wants desperately to be the very best mother possible.

Often she is determined not to repeat her own mother's mistakes; and yet at the same time she begins to understand how very difficult her mother's job was. She's also becoming aware of the great power she has in affecting her child's development. And if she has read very much at all in the area of child development, she has been told by various authorities that the mother plays one of the most critical roles in the physical, emotional, and intellectual growth of the child. Because of this, she wants to love and nurture and care for her child perfectly, and she's eager to provide the safest, healthiest, most stimulating environment she can.

But to provide this kind of environment requires tremendous emotional and physical energy, and the constant attention to the needs of another can be both exhilirating and depleting. If the woman is a single mother, the demands made of her seem particularly overwhelming. If the woman is married, and if the father is very involved in the day-to-day care of the child, her work is lessened somewhat. But even with his help the responsibilities seem tremendous, especially if the woman is like so many other women who feel the real responsibility of the child falls to them.

There's no doubt that providing for a new baby is a very

precious time for the mother. But her own needs for nurture, rest, and stimulation do not stop at delivery. The knowledgeable mother knows, too, that she must not abandon her needs, because doing so can negatively impact the relationship with her child. Jean Harsh, a social worker and respected therapist and colleague of mine in Atlanta, in working with such informed women, who know that they must also continue their own development after the birth of a child, indicates that many feel torn between these two needs.

In addition, while the woman is constantly thinking about her role as mother, she also knows that her relationship with the child's father cannot be forgotten. There's probably more interaction with other family members, too, due to the birth of the child, and even though the contact with parents, siblings, and in-laws may be good, it also can be very time consuming and sometimes draining. Because of this, the mother often begins to experience overload along with her joy. She probably feels as if she is a juggler, balancing many different roles and trying to keep them all going well.

If she has had IP fears in the past, they may emerge with greater impact than ever now. "Am I being a good mother?" she constantly asks herself. "Do I know enough about child rearing?" "Am I doing it right?" "What if I mess up?" "Will I ruin my child?" "I'm not at all sure how I should be doing this," she laments. Fear of failure. Extreme self-doubt. The need to be the best. All these Impostor symptoms come to the surface at such a time.

And if the woman is a working mother, she must also juggle one more role. Her job or career may become both a source of satisfaction and nurture as well as a real conflict. She may question how much of herself and her energy she should give to her career and how much should go to parenting. Although she may believe that working is important for her ultimate well-being and may even help her in the end to be a better mother, she probably also is having great difficulty separating herself from the child. When she was pregnant, she imagined she would be close to her baby, but the intensity of the bond she now has with her child is a tremendous surprise.

Finding quality child care is another critical issue for the working mother. She may spend a great deal of her time and energy trying to find such care and worrying about whether or not it is adequate. And if she feels the care is not good enough, her guilt may become almost overwhelming.

Of course, all these fears and concerns occur among most mothers whether they are IP victims or not. But Impostor symptoms show up when a woman doubts her ability as a mother even though there is plenty of objective evidence that her child is doing well. If there are clear indications that the child is growing, is healthy, and is fairly happy and content, and if everyone — pediatrician, teachers, relatives — except the mother admits this, then it's likely she's experiencing IP feelings in relationship to her mothering.

If she cannot believe this evidence but still feels frightened, she may be dealing with an overwhelming need to be the very best mother and a pressing need to be perfect. She may be demanding superwoman attributes of herself — qualities which no person can have *all* of the time. If this is the case, she probably is unwilling to accept help either at home or at the office — help which is desperately needed.

When I worked at a family and child guidance clinic, I saw several mothers who believed they had severe emotional problems. Generally, they had two or three preschoolers and they were providing most of the care with very little help from the fathers, other family members, or baby sitters.

On a first look, these women did indeed appear to be depressed. But a thorough interview with each woman indicated physical exhaustion instead. When I suggested that they might be suffering fatigue, they were relieved and surprised, yet at the same time self-critical. "Why can't I handle this?" they asked. "My mother did."

Most often, however, when we explored the situation more completely, it was learned that their own mothers *had* received help under similar circumstances; many had lived near an aunt or grandmother or other relative who had helped out, or they had lived in a neighborhood where friends relieved each other from time to time, providing the mothers with a few hours away from their children. The mothers who came to see me at the clinic, though, tended to live in suburban areas away from their families; they, therefore, received no help from relatives and there usually was no neighborhood network available to provide relief. These particular women also got very little assistance from their spouses, and the demands of raising the children fell almost completely on them. They felt isolated, lonely, and crazy. They also believed they were terrible mothers, and strong IP doubts emerged.

It was obvious these women needed some time to relax with no demands. It was obvious they needed help. We often were able to get the husbands much more actively involved, and we worked together to find competent child care workers and mother's-day-out programs at local churches or libraries.

In essence, we worked toward making them feel they no longer had to be superwomen. A major strategy for change was for them to get and accept help and to know that they deserved it. Next, we worked toward getting them to realize they didn't need to feel guilty for needing such help.

For women, the need to be perfect seems to occur in every aspect of their lives. They are supposed to be excellent cooks, housekeepers, lovers, mothers, wives, friends, nurturers and to be brilliant at their careers as well. Many women also believe they are never supposed to show stress or distress; they feel they're supposed to run their lives with happiness and ease. Most have a great deal of trouble saying no, and most feel they shouldn't ask for help. For years I have spoken on this topic to women audiences, and if anything, I see that the demands on women now are greater than ever. In Part Three, we'll be looking at some concrete ways for women to overcome their Impostor fears and Superwoman attitudes in regard to mothering.

THE PERFECT MALE IMAGE

In my clinical practice, I have seen many men who had to struggle with their need to be special, to be the most brilliant, the most successful — in essence to be perfect. The major difference I've seen between men and women is that men usually have these elevated standards for their jobs or careers but not for other areas of their lives, such as parenting, entertaining, or domestic responsibilities. There are indeed exceptions and some men do have the superman symptoms just as severely as superwomen, expecting themselves to be wonderful in everything they do. It's also true that social and cultural changes are beginning to cause men to experience many of the same pressures that women face, and the demands they place on themselves come from many more places than the office.

Many recent two-career marriages have created the need for both partners to share in the housework, cooking, entertaining, and parenting. And some men, usually because of divorce, are co-parenting or working as single parents. As this occurs and the men are more and more responsible for the day-to-day care of their children, all of the feelings that were described in the mothering section begin to apply to these fathers as well. They too begin to feel pulled in many directions as they try to fill all the roles that are suddenly expected of them.

PERFECTIONISM AT WORK

The atmosphere at the company where Sam worked was relaxed and generally easygoing. Yet it was not unusual for him to have anxiety attacks, headaches, and stomachaches. The pressures placed on him were totally internal and came from his perfectionistic standards and his inability to delegate work and responsibilities.

At the start of his career, Sam actually loved his job as a consultant and enjoyed developing programs for corporations and helping small companies get started. He took plenty of time with each client and carefully assessed their needs. If it took several visits with a client to make sure that client was satisfied, then that's what Sam did; and if some problem occurred, he'd work at it until it was solved and the job was absolutely complete. If Sam could have stopped here — working hard and providing excellent services — then he might have been fine.

But his company began to grow rapidly and because of his past performance, he was pressured to take on a supervisory role. In the new position, he was responsible not only for his individual clients but for all the jobs and consultants in a certain section of the city. Immediately he began to have problems. It seemed almost impossible for him to delegate work, and when he did, he became anxious and upset because so many of the employees working for him did not meet his standards. Most of these people were doing good work, but they weren't doing it as well or as flawlessly as Sam could have done. He therefore took on more and more, trying to do nearly all the jobs himself.

He also began to have severe anxiety attacks and physical ills that were brought on by his constant worry. Almost every day he feared some error would occur that would cause great losses for his clients and certain ruin for himself.

With the overload of work and the fatigue created by so much physical and mental stress, he began to feel that he was not good enough and he questioned his ability in almost every area of his job. He also began to realize that he didn't like supervisory work. But admitting this made him feel even more like a failure. In his mind, the role model of success continued further and further up the corporate ladder. And if he did not receive, or want, another promotion, then he was not living up to his image of how a man should proceed in his career.

Sam is a great example of the male IP victim who demands so much of himself in intellectual and career performances that his perfectionism actually stymies his overall goals and creates the kind of anxiety that filters down to other areas of his life. For Sam to be able to relax and again enjoy his job, he will either have to learn to delegate and accept work that may be less than perfect, or he will have to accept the fact that it's all right for him not to be promoted so quickly and not to have to accept a supervisory role. If he doesn't do one of these two things and ease up slightly, he will be doomed to constant dissatisfaction with himself, with his job, and with all those around him. And in the end, his performance will be far less impressive than it could have been.

For perfectionists, the thought of easing up and expecting less of themselves creates almost immediate panic. The reason for this fear is because of an underlying belief that they must be perfect in order to be lovable. "If I'm not perfect, no one will like me," they believe.

In Part Three, we will discuss suggestions for overcoming such fears without making the IP victim feel he or she is settling for mediocrity.

8 | Denial Of Competence And Discounting Praise

PROBABLY THE MOST dominant characteristic of IP victims is that they are unable to hear and believe the compliments of others, and they can't accept the objective evidence regarding their success or intellectual ability. Paradoxically, they desperately want to know that they're competent, well liked, and respected. Most, in fact, want to be considered brilliant and outstanding and wish they were in the genius category.

This characteristic is far from the false modesty we've all witnessed in the past: the clichéd scene where the woman is given a compliment for her dress, followed by a display of feigned modesty and her saying, "What, this old thing?" while knowing all along that the dress is indeed stunning. This characteristic also has nothing to do with the kind of people who believe they *are* brilliant and special but shrug off praise only in order to be praised all the more.

Impostors cannot accept praise because they honestly believe that the praise is not deserved. And, if anything, the praise makes IP victims feel more than ever that others have a false impression of them and that they are hiding behind an Impostor Mask. They therefore become ingenious at denying any evidence that they are bright and dismissing all verbal applause.

For instance, several IP victims I saw in therapy sessions at a prestigious college were asked, "How did you get admitted here if you lack the intelligence?" Their reply generally was, "The admissions committee made a mistake," or "I applied at a time when the number of applications received was low." When they were asked about how they were able to make such good grades, they indicated it was only because they knew how to look good on the surface and cover up all they didn't know; or they claimed they were able to charm teachers into liking them, and the good grades were due more to their personalities than their intelligence; or they stuck to the notion that they worked harder than everyone else and were therefore able to make up for their intellectual deficiencies.

Some even believed that their IQ scores and the results of standardized tests were wrong or that these tests didn't truly measure ability. "I happen to be good at multiple choice type questions," was one of the excuses I usually got. Or, when asked about their extremely high scores, they would reply, "I got lucky that day," or, "I just know how to take that kind of test." It never occurred to them that knowing how to take such an exam and score well on it was an indication that they were bright.

What these students also didn't realize was that they were indirectly saying that all those teachers and admissions committees made errors in judgment. In such cases, to help IP victims see how unlikely and even absurd it is to assume that everyone else has been wrong about their intelligence, I occasionally will make the following statement: "You must be very bright to be able to fool so many people."

It's important to remember that when Impostors give

such reasons for why they have done well, they are absolutely sincere; in their minds, it is far more plausible that an admissions committee could make an error than that they could be intellectually capable of being accepted at a good school.

In nearly every case where this particular characteristic is strong, praise not only causes a certain amount of embarrassment and a tendency on the Impostor's part to change the subject, but it truly makes the Impostor uncomfortable. It makes such people feel that once again they've fooled the world and received compliments for something that came to them because of luck or hard work. Hardly ever do these people accept the praise as a point of fact. Instead they do everything they can to dismiss the praise and discount the evidence, which should tell them that they are intelligent and creative people.

Larry, a chemist, discovered an important formula while he was looking for the solution to another problem. Rather than being proud of the discovery, he dismissed its significance, stating, "It was a fluke. I just got lucky." It's true that a certain amount of luck was involved, but Larry had the intelligence to know when he had stumbled onto an important finding rather than passing over it.

Some IP victims also believe that anything they're able to accomplish must not be very important or difficult to do. "If I can do it, there must not be so much to it," they tend to say. Harry, a very successful salesman, is a perfect example of someone with this trait. He does his work well and with ease, but because he does, he dismisses its importance. He thinks, "Anyone has the ability to do this." Yet many would fail miserably at Harry's job because they lack the verbal skills and the abilities to persuade and to understand people as he does.

Sally is another IP victim who has the misconception that if she's able to do a job, then it must be something that anyone else would be able to do. The architectural firm where she works has asked her to develop the interior structure of a new multi-million dollar office complex that is being built. This job is considered extremely important to the project directors and to her employers. Yet because Sally does interior parts of structures with ease, she totally dismisses the importance of the job. "Almost anyone could have handled this assignment," she claims.

These people attribute their successes to anything and everything except brains. Ruth, a graphics designer, received an important regional award for her work. But she dismisses the possibility that the award is an indication of her intellectual ability or talent. She is an attractive, likable, friendly person with good political skills, so she believes she has been honored because of her charm rather than her ability, and she questions the judgment of those people who have distinguished her so.

Remember, IP victims are not being coy or acting humble when they dismiss someone's praise. Inside they are afraid that they truly do not deserve the complimentary things that are being said or the awards that are being given. They also may have the superstitious idea that if they do believe the praise, something bad is likely to happen; there is the notion that if their success is acknowledged, then somehow it will disappear.

Often there's also the fear that if they accept praise for present accomplishments, then they will be expected to keep performing at the same level in the future. But if their success is considered a fluke or a matter of luck, and they aren't able to succeed again (which they believe will be the case), then they haven't expected as much of themselves and the loss isn't so great.

ACCEPTING PRAISE IS AN
ADMISSION OF GUILT

In a following chapter of this book, I discuss IP victims' fear of success and guilt about success. For people who have these concerns, it's most likely that they won't accept praise because to do so would make them have to admit that they are successful individuals. If they're able to say to themselves, "I haven't really accomplished all that much," then they've decreased some of their fear of and guilt about success.

For these people there's a real concern, too, that if they do accept the evidence that they're competent and do accept praise, then other people may be envious or may no longer like them. Students with Impostor characteristics have told me they've often pretended that they made poorer grades than they actually did in order to be accepted by their peers. And Impostors with large salaries notoriously try to hide what they make so friends won't become jealous or feel uncomfortable. One young client told me that when she was chosen "Most Likely to Succeed" at her high school and had to go before the entire student body to be recognized, she was very pleased, but at the same time she was terribly frightened and embarrassed. Again, she was afraid that accepting the award might cause her to lose her friends.

"MOTHER NEVER SAID IT, SO YOU
MUST BE WRONG."

To understand these Impostor attitudes, we need to go

back to the family dynamics discussed in the first part of this book. One of the common elements found in the family backgrounds of IP sufferers is that there is a discrepancy between the feedback received from family members and that given by teachers, employers, or friends.

In the case of Ralph, the young attorney we met in Chapters One and Four, there was very positive evidence of his intelligence from good grades, high test scores, and teachers' praise. Yet his perfectionistic father was always critical, and it seemed that Ralph could never please him. The son soon became as critical of himself as the father had been, and he, too, could find something wrong with whatever he did. So when others praised him, he could only think of all the errors he had made, and he was painfully aware of how his performance could have been improved. He also thought anyone who complimented him either was being kind or simply wasn't very astute, since it was obvious that he should have done better.

In another group of IP sufferers, the families were the opposite of critical. These families told the child, "You are brilliant. You can do anything you want to do. You can be the best — No. 1." They also tended to give very generalized praise rather than concrete, specific praise for a particular task or a particular talent. Children from such families carry a tremendous burden — thinking they should be able to do anything and everything well — and they feel intense pressure to achieve in all aspects of their lives. But when they get into the world outside their families, they learn that they are not always the best and that others are performing equally as well and sometimes better. Therefore, they become skeptical and uncomfortable with praise, especially if they know they haven't been the very best. If several thousand people receive full scholarships to schools, and they are only one among the many, they discount what they have done. The very fact that others were able to do well, too, makes them feel that they can't possibly accept praise for such a thing. They also feel fraudulent in accepting compliments for a specific accomplishment because they're afraid that the person doesn't realize they're not doing so well in other areas of their lives.

In both sets of Impostor sufferers, the families valued intelligence but rarely took the time to outwardly acknowledge and celebrate the specific tangible accomplishments of their children. Since these children want so desperately to please their families, and since they so highly regard their parents' opinions, they tend to think the praise of others is unimportant.

A key element in changing IP feelings is to change this fundamental process of denying competence and dismissing praise. In Part Three, I'll describe ways IP victims can change these symptoms and learn to believe the proof of their intelligence, which so often is right before their eyes.

9 | Fear Of And Guilt About Success

IF YOU SAW the movie *Barefoot in the Park*, you probably remember Jane Fonda saying to her on-screen husband, Robert Redford, in the midst of an argument, that he was practically perfect. Redford's character obviously took this remark as an accusation and defensively countered that it was a terrible thing to say. The dialogue makes for a humorous scene in the movie, but if it's analyzed a little more closely, it's possible that the accusation and the defensive reaction to it are more serious than appears on the surface. Robert Redford's character is afraid of being too perfect, because if he is, this separates him from his very imperfect bride. It makes him different from her, and because they're newly married and still unsure of themselves, the difference makes him feel vulnerable. If he tells himself, and her, that he isn't perfect, that he actually has as many faults as she, then he feels they are more the same, and he's less likely to lose her approval and her love.

Most people find it easy to understand an IP victim's fear of failure, but they have a far more difficult time understanding why a person would fear success and minimize the degree of the success. After all, we all want to look good in other people's eyes, so why would anyone want to downplay his or her accomplishments or try not to look successful at all? The answer is usually the same as the reason Robert Redford's character didn't want to appear perfect. Like him, these Impostors don't want to appear different, don't want to feel separated from the people they love, and, mainly, don't want to lose the affection of these people because they are different or more successful.

The most frustrating thing about this IP symptom is that although these people may fear success, at the same time they want it badly. Like the character Pip in *Great Expectations*, they are torn between desperately wanting to "be somebody" and then sometimes feeling embarrassed when they rise above possibly humble beginnings and reach that goal.

There's also another element to this particular Impostor characteristic. If we go back to *Barefoot in the Park* and look at the Robert Redford character again, we see that there is indeed a certain perfectionistic quality to this man. He does want to be the perfect attorney; he does want to be spick-and-span all the time; he does want things in order. But if he makes a claim on being perfect, this means he might not live up to the claim. If he instead declares that, "I am not!" then the demands on him aren't so great.

In much the same way, an IP victim who is afraid of success can deal with the fear more easily if he or she says, "I'm not really as successful or bright as it appears. I'm aware of how much I don't know. I know all the mistakes I've made, all my weaknesses. And I know I may not be able to repeat my past success." By taking this attitude, the Impostor doesn't expect so much of himself.

People who have such a fear of success, usually have most of the other characteristics of the Impostor Phenomenon too. Like Redford's character, they're secretly perfectionistic; or they have a tacit need to be special. But by disclaiming their perfection or their special qualities, there's far less pressure placed on them to perform or to possess these qualities. And if they don't succeed, the letdown doesn't seem so great.

Also, since in the past success usually has been associated with stress, anxiety, or real pain (due to the Impostor Cycle, the Superman/Superwoman Aspect, or other characteristics of the Impostor Phenomenon), and the victim dreads experiencing such feelings again, he or she therefore dreads success.

Impostors also may fear success because they believe they're not entitled to it. They feel they're unworthy of doing well or that they couldn't possiby deserve real success. This is all part of the IP victim's self-doubt, but there are many reasons for the intensity of such beliefs.

TOO SUCCESSFUL TOO SOON

Dr. Gail Matthews, a psychologist at Old Dominion College in San Rafael, California, found in a study of publicly successful people, that seventy percent experienced Impostor feelings and that those who had obtained success very early in their careers, at a very young age, or very rapidly, were extremely likely to have IP feelings. I have also found that those people who have reached a certain level of achievement, with what seems to be little or no effort, often experience a profound fear of success. And when success comes easily or quickly to these individuals, they find it difficult to believe or accept as being real. The result is that they usually believe the success was simply a stroke of luck, had nothing to do with them, and can't possibly be recreated again. And they're afraid that the success may disappear as rapidly as it came.

THE IMPOSTOR PHENOMENON

In truth, they may indeed have had a certain amount of luck. Yet what they forget is that they had the capacity and intelligence to utilize the good fortune that came their way and to make the most of it. They also probably had the qualifications that were needed to keep learning and to maintain the success.

LORRAINE

Unlike other children who grew up watching cartoons or Westerns, Lorraine loved the Six O'Clock News. At an incredibly early age, she knew she wanted to become one of the women television reporters standing outside the White House or the Capitol in Washington, microphone in hand, relating the national news.

She majored in broadcast journalism while in college, ranking in the top five percent of her class, and while working on her master's degree, she began work as a receptionist at one of the local TV stations. Because her older brother knew the producer of news programming at this station, she was also able to get an interview when a reporting position came open. The producer and director of the news shows were very impressed with Lorraine and decided to give her the job. It didn't take long to realize she was a natural in front of the camera. She was poised, articulate, had a keen news sense, and was a thorough reporter. In less than a year, she was promoted to the news desk and became the nightly co-anchor.

Lorraine's family was thrilled with her success and delighted that she had obtained her lifelong dream. But Lorraine felt that her success had been only a matter of luck. If her brother hadn't known the producer, if she hadn't been able to joke with him about the stories she had heard of his college days, if she hadn't been so attractive, she never would have gotten the reporting job. She even felt that her good performance as a reporter was simply good fortune; she believed she had lucked into covering some good stories that got her more attention than she actually deserved. And because she knew how long some people had to wait to be promoted to such a job, how difficult it was even to get a reporting position where she worked, she felt a sense of guilt. She felt her success had come too soon, too easily, and that she hadn't paid her dues.

As a result of these hidden feelings, when Lorraine received a call from the director of a national news network asking her to fly to New York for an interview, she was filled with fear and self-doubt. She believed that since her previous performance had been due to luck, she wouldn't possibly be able to handle the demands of such an important job. She was certain she'd make a fool of herself or show her lack of reporting savvy on national television. She was also afraid that her colleagues would talk behind her back, claiming, as she did, that her success was all the result of connections, charm, and good looks. Because of these fears, she declined the interview, using the excuse that she didn't want to live in New York.

I'M NOT ENTITLED TO SUCCESS

Other people often have the notion that somehow they're not worthwhile enough to succeed. In their minds, they don't deserve success.

Sometimes this occurs because a number of the people who are important to them haven't obtained the same degree of success. Underneath their fear is an intense guilt about having succeeded while these other people haven't.

If, for example, they're more successful than their siblings or their parents, they may feel uncomfortable with their success and want to deny it. They're also afraid that their success may make their loved ones think they're different from them or that they've changed. And, like the Robert Redford character we mentioned before, they're afraid this difference may separate them from their families or cause them to lose their parents' or siblings' love.

KATHERINE

This young woman came to me because she was having difficulty completing a college project. Even though she was employed by a federal agency doing social type work, she didn't have her degree and was going back to college to finish her education. She also hoped to obtain a graduate degree in social work. But if she couldn't complete her project, she couldn't accomplish these goals.

As we worked together on her problems, her family history emerged. She had always been close to her mother and recognized the fact that she was her mother's favorite child. Katherine knew she was intelligent, competent, and beautiful in her mother's eyes. She was pleased by this attention, but at the same time concerned that she received more love than her brothers and sisters.

In Katherine's opinion, she had been much more fortunate than her siblings. It seemed that they were either always in trouble or suffering from some crisis, and none of them was successful. And whenever she had tried to help them, it had never worked out.

She therefore began to ask such questions as, "Why should I be able to make it when they can't? I don't deserve it any more than they do." She ignored the fact that they had not made good use of help when it had been offered, and she felt totally responsible for their lack of success.

Katherine needed to experience a certain amount of sadness and even grief about their problems before she could accept and become comfortable with her own success. She had to realize that she was not responsible for their unhappiness and that she wasn't bad because her mother had loved her the most. After she worked on these issues in our therapy sessions, she was able to complete her project and her degree and allow herself to be successful without the accompanying guilt.

I MUSTN'T OUTDO DAD

Other people may impede their own progress because they have the unconscious notion that they mustn't exceed the success of their parents. And if they do outdistance their parents' success, they often harbor guilt and try to hide their accomplishments.

MILDRED

This client came into my office seeking growth-oriented therapy. She wanted to know herself better and to try to deal with the uneasy feelings she was having about the man she lived with. Shortly after therapy began, she acknowledged that she believed this man was not really in love with her. Her intuition was correct, and after a few months her lover left her for another person.

Much of the early part of her therapy centered on the loss of this relationship. Yet as we focused on ways for her to deal with the loss, the fact emerged that she felt stuck in a dead-end job. She was bright enough to handle a more demanding, promising position, but she seemed to accept where she was without question. I let her know that I thought she was smart and that I valued her intelligence. After much encouragement, she began to consider applying for a managerial position.

She received such a job and was able to handle it very competently. But before she began therapy, she never would have considered taking such a step. She had never been encouraged and no one had ever demonstrated to her that they valued her intelligence. In fact, she had received parental messages that her intelligence was unimportant; she had also gotten the message that she should not surpass her father's success.

In her new job, even though, of course, she was much younger than her father, she exceeded his annual income by several thousand dollars. This created a great deal of guilt in Mildred. She also had the unconscious fear that her family would no longer accept her if they knew she was more successful than her father. As these issues emerged in therapy, she realized that she was afraid of rejection; and possible separation from her family was something she seemed totally unable to deal with.

One of the first steps in removing all her guilt was simply to admit that the guilt was there. The next step in therapy was helping her understand that outdistancing her father's financial success had nothing to do with how much she loved him and helping her to understand that her success was not what had prevented his.

Although her family does not presently acknowledge what Mildred has accomplished, they have not rejected her either, and she feels comfortable in going home. She also came to realize that, should they ever reject her, she could survive.

10 | IP Symptoms In Special Situations

IN THE PREVIOUS chapters we have discussed not only the particular characteristics inherent in IP victims, but also the times such characteristics are most likely to show up, sending the anxiety level off the scale. We talked about those critical Impostor Prime Times, when — because of a new job, a new role as a mother or father, or beginning a career — people tend to be so overwhelmed by self-doubt that they feel immobilized and can't seem to make a decision, or they work like mad trying to make certain they don't fail.

This chapter is devoted to three groups of people who also experience most or all of the Impostor doubts. But because of different circumstances, these special situations do not fit under any of the other categories and therefore deserve a section of their own.

FIRST-GENERATION PROFESSIONALS

"Money isn't everything, you know."

The statement is one that Michael is used to hearing. This electrical engineer has a good position and considerable potential for advancement within his company. But because Michael is the only one in his family to have such a job and the first to receive a college degree, certain Impostor characteristics have emerged and are beginning to interfere with the daily enjoyment of his life.

Michael's father is a printer. His mother's a housewife. These two people are in many ways eager for their son to succeed and happy that he is more educated than they. But at times they are also very ambivalent about what he achieves. Even though Michael has given no indication that he thinks money is all-important, they still warn him about such things. Or they occasionally say to him, "Common sense is more important than book learning, Michael," even though, again, he never implies to his parents that he thinks the opposite is true.

Michael is only in his late twenties, but his parents also let him know they're disappointed that he hasn't given them the joy of grandchildren. And they let him know that they're hurt when he doesn't spend his holidays and vacations with them and when he doesn't attend weekly family dinners. They can't seem to understand that Michael travels a great deal because of his job and that it's difficult to make these weekly get-togethers. Neither are they supportive when he tries to explain that it's professionally important for him to attend company social activities instead of being with them.

From all these mixed messages, Michael is painfully aware that his parents are as frightened by his success as they are proud of it. And he naturally feels a conflict over what his parents want of him and what is expected of him professionally. Since his kind of work is so foreign to them, he also finds it difficult to really talk with them about what he's doing; but at the same time they feel left out when he doesn't tell them what's going on at the office.

Since starting his job, Michael has become good friends with a co-worker named Chris. Both of Chris's parents are successful professionals — his father's a newspaperman and his mother is a social worker — and Chris is able to talk with them about any number of issues, matters that Michael would never be able to discuss with his family. Michael is envious of the easy relationship and exchange of ideas that Chris has with his parents and the pride they show over their son's independence and accomplishments.

What Michael fails to see, however, is that he has an excitement and enthusiasm about his career and is thrilled about each new professional step he takes. In contrast, his friend Chris takes these matters for granted and doesn't have Michael's energy or drive. But because Michael feels that he moves in two worlds — that of his parents and that concerning his professional life — Michael experiences Impostor feelings and a good deal of turmoil.

Michael's therapy work centers on getting him to recognize the mixed messages he is receiving from his family and to realize those messages are part of the reason he feels so pulled apart. He's also encouraged to talk more with his parents and to give them information about what's going on at work, even if they don't understand, and to let them know about all the expectations and demands that are made on him there. He's encouraged, too, to express how much he loves and appreciates them. Their main fear has been that because Michael is educated and successful, he will leave them behind. Yet the more they pull on him, the more likely he is to want distance from them. Therefore, when he gets mixed messages, he's asked to gently confront his parents. For example, when they express their disappointment and lack of understanding when he doesn't get home for a week at Christmas, he's encouraged to say, "As I've explained, I can't take that time off from my work because it's a critical period in my business — a time when I'm badly needed. Do you want me to get in trouble at work?"

If his parents say no, that of course they don't want him to jeopardize his position, then he can add, "Well, I feel conflict when you ask me to do something that I can't do because of my job. It puts me in a bind." It's probable that his parents never realized they were putting him in such a predicament, and when he gently lets them know his feelings, they're likely to change.

First-generation professionals often have a great deal of guilt about their success, mainly because they don't want to make the ones they love feel uncomfortable or somehow less important or less intelligent. And at the same time they very much want to excel and want to learn and be all they can. The film *Educating Rita*, about a working-class British woman who sets out to receive a college education, treats these issues in an entertaining, humorous way. But even though the movie is a comedy, it shows the real conflicts such people can have when they begin moving in different circles and in different directions from the people they've known all their lives. They often feel they are caught in the middle, unlike those they've left behind and yet still not really like the people who have become their colleagues or peers.

FINDING A MENTOR

The other important part of Michael's therapy was to encourage him to find a mentor — someone who could teach him the ropes and the unwritten rules of the professional world. First-generation professionals can especially benefit from listening to people who are successful and who probably have a greater understanding of what the younger person is going through and what it takes to make it in a demanding field. I encourage my clients who are in this category to seek out such people and accept their help. Many older professionals enjoy the role of mentor and can provide valuable information and knowledge; of course, it's important to find people who are self-confident enough not to be threatened by the aspiring younger career person.

Michael found such a mentor — a man named Randy who taught him how to make the best use of the resources and networks that were available in their company. Michael soon learned the best way to get his ideas and work noticed by superiors, and through Randy he made valuable new contacts. He was also able to ask Randy's advice and opinions on matters he wouldn't discuss with his family — personal and social matters such as which wine to choose, how to buy clothes, where to vacation, and so forth.

Even though first-generation professionals such as Michael usually have been encouraged and supported in their endeavors by at least some members of their families, it's still important for them to have role models and people with whom they can discuss their professional fears and worries. Without such interchange, their lack of experience and their feelings of isolation may create additional self-doubts and raise even more Impostor-type questions.

CHILDREN OF THE EXCEPTIONAL, SUPER-SUCCESSFUL FAMILIES

When a family has had a history of outstanding success or one of the parents has become noted or famous, there is a different kind of pressure on children. They ask, "Can I be as good as Mom or Dad?" "Can I live up to the family image?" "What if I *don't* measure up?"

In Rose Kennedy's book, *Times to Remember*, she recalls how her husband Joe used to say to their children that he wanted no losers, that in their family they wanted winners. The Kennedy children faired all right and indeed did turn out to be the leaders and winners that their parents expected. But some children of such successful families, who have the opportunity to attend the best schools and have the advantages of money and travel, often fear that they can't live up to all they've been given. "What if I fail when I have so many advantages?" they constantly ask themselves.

There's also the reality that it may be difficult to do as well as or better than a high-achieving parent. And even when individuals from this type of family do gain recognition or fame or success, they may still have doubts about themselves, asking the question, "Did I succeed because of my abilities or because my family is so well known?" Since this question is difficult to be objective about and difficult to answer, Impostor-type fears are apt to arise.

If individuals from such successful backgrounds have a strong need to be the very best or to be the most special, then they are especially prone to suffer IP feelings: it's difficult for them ever to believe they're as special or as outstanding as the famous parent. In addition, if the parents are very critical or perfectionistic, the children are more likely than ever to become fault-finding of themselves while trying to do everything perfectly.

These children also often struggle with individuality and have difficulty finding ways they can be unique. If they decide to stay in the same fields or areas of expertise as their well-known mothers or fathers, they are afraid of being constantly compared to the parents. Yet at the same time, they may feel there is no other path for them to take since they have similar interests and abilities. Hank Williams, Jr., has written in his songs about being compared with his famous father, yet this man is certainly talented in his own right. Still, he is criticized by some if he imitates Hank Williams, Sr., and criticized by others if he tries to be different. If such people have had IP feelings as children, their self-doubts will be more apparent than ever when they try to find a niche for themselves as adults. And if they attempt to go their separate ways and enter an entirely different field from their successful parents, they may be afraid of displeasing or letting down their families.

George is a perfect example of someone with such a history. When he entered therapy, he was suffering from intense IP feelings. He was anxious, somewhat depressed, indecisive, and unable to move toward pursuing the career he wanted. George's grandfather years before had started a business that became a national corporation of immense financial success. The business in turn made the family quite wealthy and famous. George's father, who loved the business, the money, and the power, had continued the success by stepping into the grandfather's role and becoming the corporate president.

The family business had been started in a medium-sized city, and, because it employed thousands there, everyone knew who George was. They also knew he had the best tutors and that he attended the finest schools and camps. If he wanted anything, he generally got it. Both parents also gave George a great deal of attention, and his mother thought he was brilliant and believed he could accomplish anything. In his early teens, due to his intelligence and sensitivity, he became aware of all the advantages he was receiving. He also became aware of the fact that he was expected to be brilliant and to carry on the family tradition.

But George had no interest in business or the corporate world. He loved music; and with his talents and the best lessons and much practice, he was becoming a fine jazz pianist. Yet he often felt blocked in his work. He had intense doubts about his ability even though his teachers told him he had potential. As he thought more and more seriously about becoming a professional musician, his IP feelings increased.

Could he dare not follow in his father's footsteps? he asked himself. If he did dare such a thing, he was terrified he might fail and thus upset and disappoint his family. And even if he succeeded, he would never make a fortune, he knew, and might not gain fame.

Only after intensive, long-term therapy work was George able to risk going his own way. Although he did not become famous, his music became intrinsically rewarding to him and he was able to lead a productive, happy life.

STUDENTS

The type of demands placed on students seems to create conditions which contribute to an increase in IP behaviors and feelings. Students tend to score higher on the Impostor Test than any other group. This is probably because they are regularly being graded or evaluated, and on the basis of these evaluations, decisions are made that will profoundly affect their lives and determine whether they can proceed toward their goals.

The higher the level of education they reach — such as graduate programs and professional schools — the more students are made to demonstrate that they have learned specific procedures and skills as well as theoretical knowledge. For instance, clinical psychologists may be required to demonstrate that they are effective psychotherapists and diagnosticians by submitting psychotherapy transcripts and psychodiagnostic assessments for evaluation of their clinical work. Physicians and dentists must prove their competence in diagnosis and treatment of patients. Artists and musicians often must show evidence of their training and proficiency by having shows, designing portfolios, and giving recitals.

And even after these people complete their degrees and fulfill all of their requirements, they may face standardized examinations in order to be qualified or licensed to practice their professions. There are numerous points all along the way where they may be told, "No, you do not qualify." "You can't proceed." "You can't graduate unless . . ."

For people with IP traits, this process of constant evaluation is painful and anxiety-filled. "Am I good enough?" "Can I make it?" "What do I really know?" are questions they repeatedly ask themselves. Because of their terror of failure, their need to be the best or to be perfect, their tendency to underestimate and doubt their abilities, and their propensity to remember only their deficits and forget their strengths, IP victims often find being a student one of the most difficult times of their lives.

Blanche is an example of such a person. She was an attractive, articulate, twenty-five-year-old woman who consulted me because she wanted to become a psychologist. And although she would have no problem being admitted to the university where she wanted to attend graduate school, she was afraid to apply because she had suffered so much in college. She had agonized over every test and every paper while in undergraduate school, and she felt she couldn't face another six or seven years of such torment. Because her college experience had been so painful, she knew she must change before embarking on any further educational pursuits.

Since she was so motivated to change her Impostor behaviors, she practiced coping strategies over and over again. She has subsequently been accepted to a graduate program at a major university, and with less frequent IP feelings she is able to enjoy being a student and is much more confident that she will succeed.

In Part Three we'll discuss ways to overcome Impostor feelings that will be particularly valuable for students and, as in the case of Blanche, greatly increase their enjoyment of these school years.

11 | The IP Victim And Relationships

IT'S NEARLY TWO A.M., and Beverly sits huddled in a corner of the sofa. She's been working round the clock for days now, trying to get ready for a one-woman show at a local art gallery. She's barely left her house, where she also has her studio, and the only person she has seen is her husband Michael.

She's been irritable and cranky, she knows, even though she tried hard not to be, and she's snapped at Michael far more times than she meant to. But she has been so worried about this show, so anxious about what the critics and the buyers may think, and she's terrified that she won't have produced enough good work. She might have worked far into the night if Michael hadn't come to the door of her studio and urged her to come to bed. Now she sits this way on the sofa, sipping a glass of wine to relax but still too tired and too keyed up to go to sleep.

Michael walks over to her, kneads her shoulder, and says, "Please don't do this to yourself again."

"I don't know what you mean," she says much more sharply than she had meant.

"Yes you do. You're absolutely miserable, and you're worrying yourself to death over this one show."

"Well, you would too, if your work was this bad."

"Beverly, your work is wonderful."

"You say that because you love me."

"I say that because it's true. Everyone thinks so. Everyone tells you so, Bev."

"Well, I don't think so. It's never good enough. I know I always should have done better. I don't even know why this gallery keeps inviting me back."

"They invite you back because your shows always produce at least a seventy-five percent sellout."

"I think the owner feels sorry for me. You know she knew my dad."

"Oh, I give up. I just simply give up," Michael says, and stomps off to bed.

Beverly picks up the clean paint brush she had placed on the coffee table in front of her, runs its bristles across her hand, and, even though she knows she's probably made Michael mad, decides maybe she should go back to her studio and work just a little while more.

This scenario is a predictable one in Beverly and Michael's home. She is the artist we met in Chapter One who, although she has gained a fine reputation, is always terrified before a show. She has trouble sleeping before such an event, and she can be short-tempered, touchy, and a downright difficult person with whom to live. Her husband, Michael, agonizes with her and has made many, many attempts to reassure her about her work. But she will not believe him when he tells her how wonderful he thinks her paintings are, and she often, because she thinks she's being pampered or patronized, becomes even more irritable when he tries.

After her shows, when Michael wants to celebrate her success, she often is still unhappy over some incident or comment that has or has not been made. A fellow artist, during one of her shows, said nothing to her about her paintings, and she was certain he hated them but simply had said nothing in order to spare her feelings. So that night following the show, when she and Michael went to a favorite restaurant to celebrate, rather than recalling all the complimentary things that were said to her and thinking about the large number of sales that had been made, she thought instead about this one man. She couldn't get it out of her mind that he hated her work, and, as much as she tried to be cheerful, the celebration was ruined. Later the next week, she received a congratulatory note from this artist, saying how much he had enjoyed the show and how much he admired her new work. Her first reaction was to hold the note up to Michael and ask, "Did you say something to him? Did you ask him to send this note because I was upset?" In disbelief, and totally frustrated, Michael could only shake his head.

Later she realized that of course her husband wouldn't have done such a thing, and she realized the artist had more integrity than to write a letter to her about something he didn't truly believe. She realized how silly her reaction and her comment had been. But the reaction had been genuine — nothing contrived or the tantrum of a spoiled brat. Beverly's lack of confidence in her success was so intense that she truly believed no one else could possibly think such good things about her work.

She often wondered how Michael could tolerate her moods, her constant self-doubt, and her visible turmoil. And even though she knew he loved her, she also had some fears that he might leave her when he discovered how incompetent she really was. In truth, Michael did love her very much, and her Impostor fears and traits did not jeopardize their marriage. But it did test their relationship at times and often made Michael feel that he was helpless in dealing with his wife's doubts.

THE SYMPATHETIC OTHER

When someone lives with, loves, or is a very close friend or colleague of an IP victim, that person begins to see all of the characteristics that we've discussed regarding the Impostor profile. In the initial stages of the relationship, however, he or she more than likely was not aware of the fears of the IP sufferer because the person probably came across as confident, energetic, and somewhat self-assured. The friend or lover probably was impressed with this self-assurance and the accomplishments of the Impostor. Only after the IP victim begins to trust the friend or lover, and is willing to let that person know him or her better, is the chronic self-doubt discovered.

After the partner has seen the real person behind the mask, the IP victim is more likely to admit how afraid he or she is of certain situations. "I'm really worried about taking this test." "I don't think I can give that speech." "I'll never be able to get through this interview with the president." "You know, of course, that I'll never get this job. Why should I? I don't even know why I'm trying." And not only do Impostors make such statements, they begin to show their anxiety. The friend or lover begins to notice the sweaty palms, the pounding heart, the flushed face; he becomes aware of the lack of sleep, the distress in the voice, the panicked work patterns.

The first time or two these episodes occur, the partner may also experience real concern that the other person will fail. Yet the IP victim generally comes back having not failed at all, but having succeeded.

A speech was given — the response was excellent, the applause was loud.

A test was taken — the IP victim received an A.

An interview was given — the Impostor got the job.

After seeing such success, the partner usually is relieved and happy. But the next time the Impostor Cycle occurs (generally because the IP victim is so intense about how badly he or she expects to do and so genuine about the fear), the partner may also feel frightened and concerned again. But by the third or fourth time such occurrences are witnessed, the partner begins to say, "Wait a minute. Last time you went through the same thing, and you did fine. You *always* do fine. And you'll do fine this time, too."

"But you don't understand," the IP victim replies. "This time is different. This time I really don't know the material. *This* time I really may fail."

The partner tries to understand and tries to be supportive and encouraging, but in spite of the efforts, the cycle is repeated once again. Now the partner tries even harder to reassure the IP victim, to give praise and point out all of the individual's strengths. But the Impostor dismisses the praise — probably dismisses it even more quickly or more thoroughly than the praise given by someone else. "You're just biased because you love me and care about me," is a common response. Or, "You're just being kind." And, "You're afraid to tell me the truth or to criticize."

Even after constant reassurances, the IP victim finds it almost impossible to believe the positive things the partner says. Partly because of the victim's family history, in which there was a discrepancy in the responses that were received from the outside world and those received at home, the Impostor still expects a discrepancy; and therefore he or she continues to dismiss the praise and reassurances of lovers and friends, just as he or she has dismissed it in other places, because it probably is different from what's being received from family members.

After seeing the Impostor Cycle being repeated and after realizing that encouragement does little good, friends and lovers often become frustrated and angry and think, "Why can't you just see that you're good? Why can't you enjoy this?" And if these supportive people aren't experiencing as much success in their own lives, they're likely to lose patience and think, "If I had that kind of success, I'd appreciate it." Or if they have gained their own success, they still may be frustrated and impatient and say, "I enjoy my success, so why can't you do the same? This should be such a great time in our lives. I just don't understand."

If the patterns continue, the partner or friend simply may give up and withdraw or wish to leave. They may think, "Nothing I can say or do helps, so I'm going to quit trying!" They feel helpless and somewhat hopeless. And when the IP victim recognizes this type of withdrawal, instead of acting on it, he or she usually feels worse than ever and more full of self-doubt.

When the IP victim responds to the withdrawal with pain, the partner generally tries again. But if some change does not take place, the partner is likely to withdraw again and refuse to deal with the person's IP feelings.

THE FRUSTRATED OTHER

Another problem that partners of IP victims report is that they're often unable to discriminate between when the Impostors are truly in trouble and actually *may* fail, and when they're simply once again going 'round and 'round on the Impostor Cycle. They've heard "Wolf!" cried so many times that it's difficult for them to know when something is really going poorly. And they may become so frustrated that after awhile they pay no attention to any of it.

They also indicate that they're afraid to be critical of their partners, and that they find it difficult to tell them anything they do not like. Yet if the IP victims pick up on the fact that they're being dishonest or holding back criticism, their worst fears — that others simply are being nice — have come true. So another kind of cycle occurs, one where the partners are afraid to be critical and afraid to hold back at the same time. They begin to feel that almost anything they say or do will be taken the wrong way or will increase their loved one's fears and self-doubts.

A further frustration for partners comes after success, when IP victims can't seem to celebrate or enjoy what they've achieved. Because these victims tend to concentrate on the one error or the one flaw of a performance, they can't seem to forget it and take joy in all the good that occurred. If they worked on a project that was ninety-nine percent perfect and one percent flawed, IP sufferers are likely to concentrate on the one percent and dismiss all that they did so well. By dwelling on the part that they felt was imperfect, they're far from being in a mood to celebrate. And when their partners are eager to finally relax and toast the success, tensions are apt to occur.

Having trouble celebrating also may dovetail with another personality trait of most Impostors. Dr. Norma Lawler, a psychotherapist in San Jose, California, has done research demonstrating that IP victims are much more likely to have introverted rather than extroverted personalities. Introverts tend to be thoughtful persons who pay close attention to their feelings. They often appear preoccupied and may feel somewhat uncomfortable interacting with people in large groups (although with IP victims this is usually disguised, and only people who are extremely close to them realize how uncomfortable and shy they truly are). Extroverts, who are less likely to experience IP fears, are action-oriented, problem-solving people. In my clinical experience, I have found that introverted people who experience strong IP feelings have a decided tendency to pick these more gregarious individuals as partners and friends. And although extroverts generally pick introverts as partners, often to help slow them down, the extreme differences in their personalities can present problems. If the IP victims seem never to be able to celebrate their successes, but instead withdraw more than ever to dwell on their perceived failures, the more gregarious partners become increasingly frustrated, angry, and less likely to be understanding. They can't comprehend why their partners *simply don't do* something about the way they feel, or why they can't seem to change easily.

BRINGING PERFECTIONISM TO THE RELATIONSHIP

Most of the time, the real fears that IP victims have about not being good enough or not being perfect are confined to intellectual or career pursuits. But occasionally these fears spill over into their relationships with others.

I indicated earlier that new mothers may begin to have fears regarding their children. They tend to ask themselves repeatedly, "Am I a good mother?" "Am I doing all I can for my child?" "Am I doing this the best way?" They ask themselves these questions even when there is obvious evidence that their children are fine and that they are excellent mothers. In much the same way, IP fears can surface in their relationships with their spouses, lovers, or friends. They begin asking the same kinds of quesions: "Am I a good wife?" "Am I a good enough friend?" "Am I giving as much to this marriage as I should?" The other person in the relationship may insist that things are fine and that they're happy in their marriage or partnership. But IP victims have trouble believing these messages, and the same kind of dynamics that surround their successes begin to surround their relationships. Often when this occurs, reassurances again do not work well, and counseling may be required. Sometimes, however, IP victims are better able to hear the positive reinforcement and reassurances of those they love after they've been together for some while, after they become more and more convinced that their partners are going to remain with them, and after they've been shown in overt ways how very much they are loved.

Often, though, because they're so afraid of losing love and because they so much want to be perfect partners, IP victims may try very hard to please others. They may go to great efforts to care for people and to protect them and to make sure that their feelings are never hurt. They also may begin to feel that they're responsible for other people's happiness and sense of well being. They begin to think that maybe if they are perfect enough, they can make other people happy. Yet because they cannot keep up their own standards of perfection, they may feel inadequate in a relationship and begin to fear that they're no longer loved or respected. At the same time, as much as the relationship may mean to them, they often begin to resent all the time and energy they're devoting to it — even though their partners have never asked for such efforts.

RELATIONSHIPS WITH PARENTS

As I indicated in Part One of this book, there is often a discrepancy in what the families of IP victims say and think about them and what other people in authority say and think. This kind of discrepancy can affect and sometimes damage the relationship between IP victims and their parents.

If the parents are the type who chose another child as the family's star, they often ignore or deny the accomplishments of the Impostor or act as if these achievements are unimportant. When the IP victims try to discuss their success, the parents often change the subject and act disinterested. The victims feel hurt, confused, and often angry. They don't understand why their parents don't get excited about their successes but do seem excited about those of another offspring. The victims, because of their wounded feelings, may withdraw and begin to visit parents less.

In therapy, I ask clients to gently confront such parents. For instance, they might say, "When I talk about my work, you always change the subject. Are you not interested in what I'm doing?" Generally the parents are shocked and say that, of course, they're interested in their child. But even those who do not demonstrate immediate concern usually become more aware of how they've been responding. Most times these parents aren't conscious of their behavior, and a confrontation almost always makes them begin to listen.

Some parents of Impostors don't simply ignore or deny accomplishments but are overtly hostile or critical of them. They may make such statements as, "If I'd had your advantages, I could have accomplished what you have, and maybe more," or, "Success isn't everything. Don't forget that." They may also find the IP victim's most vulnerable areas and continually pick at them.

One such parent often said to her daughter, who had become a TV camera operator, "I can't believe you got all that education just to operate a camera." And a father complained to his son, who was a teacher, "Your brother makes four times the money you do, and he didn't go to college."

Even though IP victims are deeply hurt by this criticism, they desperately long for the love and approval of their parents. They usually return again and again, often with more achievements under their belts, hoping that this time their parents finally will approve of them or respond in a positive way. Unfortunately, these particular parents rarely do. They often feel competitive with or angry at the Impostor. These parents often have serious problems of their own, but they rarely recognize or admit the problems or their pain, and they're not likely to seek professional help.

As IP victims begin to change their own behaviors and understand the source of their Impostor feelings, they gradually admit that they are not likely to get the approval they seek at home. When this happens, they can begin to work toward winning the approval of others and finding substitute parents or role models for themselves.

Frequently, they begin making their visits and contacts

with these caustic parents very brief. When the parents notice the withdrawal, many of them become upset and want to know what has happened. If they're deeply concerned, some are willing to participate in family therapy, where they have a tendency to listen to the therapist on matters that they would not discuss openly with the child. Others become only hurt or angry, refusing to communicate or to change, and the gap between them and their children only grows wider.

Another kind of relationship exists between IP victims and those parents who say their children are wonderful, outstanding, and able to do anything they want to do. The problem here is that Impostors know they can never live up to the expectations of their parents, and yet they try over and over again to please them. They also probably try to protect their parents and never let them know if they have problems or suffer from Impostor fears and guilts. And they're afraid that their parents will no longer love them if they discover they are not wonderful or perfect at all times.

These parents also tend to give generalized praise. "Johnny, you can be whatever you want to be. You can do anything," they say. But they never give Johnny specific praise or openly celebrate a particular triumph. They believe their child does everything with ease and never think to tell him they've noticed how hard he works. These parents often brag about their child to others and assume the child knows they're proud of him, and they're genuinely shocked when the child says he believes he can never please them.

One of my clients was an actress who was beginning to gain acclaim and recognition, yet she believed she could never gain the approval of her mother. In a session with this woman and her mother, she told her mother how much she needed her love and approval. The mother was surprised and said, "But you always looked so competent and strong, I didn't think you needed me."

IP victims with such backgrounds are encouraged to tell their parents about their Impostor feelings. When they hear their children's fears and concerns, parents often are able to change in positive ways.

RELATIONSHIPS WITH SIBLINGS

Although relationships with siblings generally are not as critical or as intense as those with parents, they still are very important. If, for example, another child in the family was designated as the special one, IP victims may experience jealousy or feel distant toward that sibling. Impostors may also secretly resent the parents for creating a gap between their children.

But, on the other hand, if IP victims are far more successful than the other children in their families, they may experience tremendous guilt and have difficulty being themselves around these family members. They may feel they are responsible for their happiness and welfare and be constantly disappointed if they do not do well in life. The siblings may also be jealous of or intimidated by IP victims' success and equally as uncomfortable around them.

Occasionally a sibling who has been very critical of an IP victim serves the same role as an overly critical parent and can have just as much of an effect. The same kinds of dynamics occur with the sibling as with caustic or critical parents, and IP victims usually try to protect themselves by dealing with the brother or sister as little as possible.

The most noticeable element in relationships with both parents and siblings is that Impostors, because they have been hurt or criticized by these people, because they feel they can never please or live up to expectations, or because they feel guilty that they have done better financially, scholastically, or careerwise, distance themselves from those they truly love. They feel separated and lonely and often believe that they aren't wanted by or don't belong with the rest of the family. If the feelings are very intense and the hidden resentments and lack of communication have lasted for many years, it may be difficult or impossible to bridge the gap between the Impostor and his or her family without professional help.

~ ~ ~

There are many other factors which affect the quality of a relationship besides an individual's IP behavior, and I am not saying that IP victims are more likely to have dysfunctional relationships than other people. I'm simply describing the types of interactions that I have seen occur in connection with the Impostor Phenomenon.

In general, I have found that IP victims, since they usually are bright, energetic, hardworking people, are very willing to work at their relationships. They usually also are the types of people who are liked, loved, and respected, and their partners and friends are generally willing to tolerate their behaviors and work with them toward change.

If you are an IP victim, in the next three chapters we will discuss positive ways of working toward such change. And if you are the friend, spouse, lover, or relative of an Impostor, you'll probably be interested in reading Chapter Fifteen, which gives suggestions for helping these sensitive people.

Taking Off The Mask

12 | Examining The Mask And Breaking The Cycle

IF YOU RECALL back in Chapter Four, when we first took a look at the Impostor Mask, we saw that it had the look of self-assurance, of confidence, of being in control. The person wearing the mask, like most Impostors, was probably a very likable, pleasant person who had good social skills and seemed happy and appeared at ease. In fact, you probably would never have guessed that this person was suffering or feeling inadequate at all.

But from what we've discussed so far, it's obvious that the people hiding behind such masks are apprehensive and distressed to the point that their IP feelings have prevented a sense of well-being, causing them to be counterproductive at times. IP feelings have decreased the enjoyment of what they have accomplished. As a result, these IP victims generally are eager to change their behaviors and remove the mask. Many have tried in the past to do just that; some of their methods may have worked, but chances are, most have failed.

One of the reasons for this failure is that it's highly likely they've never had a label for the symptoms they've experienced. Although their fears and worries are very real to them, they've probably never said, "I'm having impostor

129

feelings. I'm always thinking that I have to mask who I am." Once they are able to say such things, most Impostors feel that there might be hope. They're usually deeply relieved to find out that they're not alone and that the Impostor experience occurs very frequently among many intelligent, successful people. This knowledge in itself may change the sense of shame and secrecy that surrounds so many IP victims.

Therefore, to begin the recovery of the Impostor Phenomenon and to take the first steps toward removing the Impostor's Mask, it's necessary to further examine that mask and to admit that it exists. The following instructions may be helpful in doing so. (In this part of the book, there will be several exercises that were found to be highly effective in the workshops originated and conducted by Clance and Imes.)

- Get a small notebook that fits into a pocket or purse and can be easily carried with you most of the time. Whenever you find yourself doubting your ability to cope, to complete a task, or your ability to succeed, make a note about such feelings and what you're saying to yourself at the time. In looking over these notes, try to determine if what you're experiencing fits with what you've read so far about Impostor feelings. See if you *are* running on the Impostor Cycle whenever you face a new challenge; determine if you *are* experiencing the "Need to be Special" whenever you're around other competitive, bright individuals; watch and see if you *do* deny or dismiss those things you've done well or *do* negate your capacity to succeed; be honest about whether your need to be perfect *does* prevent you from enjoying the things you accomplish or perhaps prevents you from reaching higher goals. If you find that you are having such Impostor feelings, label them accordingly. If you have a "Fear of Success," say so. Knowing that these feelings are Impostor symptoms and that they do not represent a valid, realistic assessment of your abilities is important.

- In this same notebook, write down not only how you felt under these circumstances, but how you actually performed. For example, if you recently started a new job and wrote that you indeed went through the Impostor Cycle and that you were terrified of failing in some way, also write down whether you actually *did* fail or whether you are progressing very well. Study this list and then try from now on not to use your feelings of doubt and anxiety as indications of your performance, but use the actual performance as an indication instead.

If in the past you've done well and have been successful most of the time, tell yourself that these experiences represent your true ability. Trust what actually has happened rather than believing your IP feelings. Many of my clients have found that they can begin to say, "Even though I'm feeling scared and doubtful about my abilities, I have conclusive proof (here on paper) that I have always done well in the past, and I therefore know I can repeat such a performance again. I have Impostor feelings, but they are doubts that are not reality-based. The truth is that I do succeed." As these clients have become aware of their IP feelings, they have gained the power to change them.

- Now try something else. As you undergo similar circumstances, think about whether you feel as if you're approaching people and projects naturally, as yourself, or whether you're wearing an Impostor Mask. For example, if you tend to be guilty about or fear success, the next time you're around people you love but who perhaps aren't so successful, decide whether or not you downplay your own accomplishments. Do you try to prevent them from knowing how much money you make or how far you've gotten in your job? Do you try to keep them from knowing that you've recently won an award? Instead of acting the way you might around your colleagues or friends, do you act unnaturally to try to be more like these other people? In other words, really take a close look at the way you talk and act around these people and determine if you're wearing an Impostor Mask. If you find that you are, then the next time you're around these same people, try slipping the mask away a little at a time, and try being more yourself. Imagine how much more comfortable you would be without the mask and what a relief it would be to finally admit how you actually feel. And imagine how others would react if they saw the more vulnerable, more human face that's been hiding so long under the synthetic one. Be realistic about this and try to decide if they would react as harshly or dramatically as you've always feared. But the most important thing is to first admit whether or not you actually do often hide behind such a mask and conceal your real feelings.

If you find that you do, then take your daily activities one at a time — conferences you participate in, memos you write, discussions with the boss, starting a difficult assignment, etc. — and log them in your notebook.

Then go back through the list and write beside each one either "Mask" or "Mask-free," according to the way you handled each activity. If you had to write a series of memos and you admitted that they weren't as important as other items waiting on your desk and therefore you dashed them off quickly, write beside that activity, "Mask-free." But if, because you were afraid of appearing imperfect, you edited and rewrote each memo a couple of times, making sure there were no mistakes, spending far more effort on them than was necessary, write beside this activity, "Mask." After you've gone through the list, go back through it one last time and see how often you felt yourself wearing an Impostor Mask. Again, becoming aware of such tendencies and such feelings is the first step in becoming more permanently "Mask-free!"

JANET

This is the woman we mentioned earlier who worked with a federal agency and who, although she had received many awards for her outstanding service, negated these honors. "I happened to be in the right place at the right time, and I know all the right people," she said not only to herself but to others.

But as Janet recognized her Impostor feelings and her denial of her assets, she began to realize that her dismissal was also a negation of the people who presented her with the awards. She began to recognize that knowing the right people may have helped her get the awards but that these people certainly wouldn't have chosen her for recognition unless she had demonstrated real competence and the ability to work exceptionally well with others. She began to acknowledge that her capacity to impress others and to develop good working relationships was the result of creative intelligence. Reaching such conclusions came only after admitting to herself that she had Impostor feelings, putting labels on those feelings, and admitting, too, that a great deal of her time was spent behind an Impostor Mask.

UNDERSTANDING THE IMPOSTOR CYCLE

In Chapter Five we discussed in detail the vicious Impostor Cycle that often takes place when IP victims face new projects or take on new duties. Briefly, to restate it, after the Impostor accepts such a project or job, he or she begins to experience:

> Bad Dreams/Worry/Fear — Immobility/Procrastination or Overpreparation — Frenzied Work — Success — Praise — Temporary Relief.

Yet the next time he or she faces another task, the success of the previous project is denied, and the fear, self-doubt, and worry are repeated all over again.

It's important for people who have developed such patterns to understand the superstitious behavior that occurs, thus convincing them that it's neccessary to worry and doubt and feel anxiety or panic in order to do well. It's important to understand, too, how the success that occurs actually reinforces the whole cycle, making the Impostor very wary of change.

BREAKING THE CHAIN

For people who've found themselves believing that such

a pattern of living and working is necessary, in order to really break the chain they need to be willing to creatively experiment with changing aspects of the cycle. I've found that the following exercises have been helpful in such cases.

- As you look at the projects and activities that are facing you in the future (such as giving a speech, writing a brief, entertaining the boss, composing an important letter, taking an exam), pick one that you've always been successful at in the past. If you ordinarily worry four or five days in advance of such an activity, decide that this time you will allow yourself to fret for only one or two days. If you start to worry prematurely, tell yourself to stop and switch your thoughts to something else. This may be difficult at first, but be firm, and don't let yourself fall into the usual pattern ahead of time. Then be sure to follow through with your activity. You'll probably discover that you've succeeded not without a total lack of worry, but that you *have* succeeded with far less agony than is normal for you. If this experiment works, decide to repeat it with a similar activity soon. This time, limit your "worry allotment" to an even shorter period.

- What we fantasize or imagine about ourselves affects us very powerfully. Therefore, in this next exercise, try to imagine yourself going through a particularly anxiety-arousing situation without all the accompanying fear and doubt. Picture yourself being confident and competent. Say to yourself, "I've done this in the past a hundred times, and I can do it again with no problem." If you have trouble with this fantasy, ask yourself if there are reasons you need to keep your Impostor traits; do you feel safe only as long as you worry and fret? Make a list of any advantages you may get from hiding behind an Impostor Mask.

CHANGING THE FRENZIED WORK PATTERN

Because of a need to be special or perfect and an overall fear of failure, many Impostors spend an excessive amount of time and thought on certain kinds of tasks that actually come to them very easily or could be accomplished with little preparation. If they've followed the normal pattern of the Impostor Cycle and procrastinated before attempting a project, these people are especially apt to work like demons trying to make up for lost time; and in the end, because of exhaustion or panic, they're likely to be less prepared than if they'd gone about the project calmly, spending the minimal amount of time and energy to do it well.

For people who have a tendency to be overprepared and to spend far more effort on tasks than is necessary, the following experiment has proved to be helpful.

• Pick out a task that is not crucial to your job or your personal situation. Deliberately spend less time and effort on this task than you ordinarily would. Watch yourself closely and allow only the amount of hours necessary to do the job well. Again, as in the first exercise, proceed with the project and see what happens to you. If you're able to succeed with less work, you can begin to systematically decrease the amount of time needed in different aspects of your performance. But if you find that you simply are unable to back off and try less hard, ask yourself why. What would have happened if you had not worked so hard? What would have happened if you had spent three hours on the task instead of an entire day? Would the project have been a fiasco? If you admit that it probably wouldn't have been, then try once again.

MARIE

Back in Chapter Five, we discussed a young woman named Marie, who headed an important program for a state agency and for whom occasionally it was necessary to deliver speeches. It was normal for her to begin her feelings of panic at least two weeks before such a speech and then to proceed through the entire vicious Impostor Cycle. In therapy she was asked to fantasize being successful at giving a speech but without going through all the days of agony. We worked together to determine how many hours she really needed to spend getting ready for such a task in order to be well prepared. At first she changed the cycle by worrying only one week instead of two. Gradually she decreased even further the amount of time she worried, and she did not frantically overprepare. Now she does not panic at all when she must give a speech. She has a realistic estimate of how prepared she needs to be and sticks to that amount. Of course, she still experiences some excitement and anticipatory anxiety right before her speeches; but a manageable amount of anxiety is good, she has learned, and her work now gives her pleasure with a minimal amount of pain.

In Marie's case, it was helpful to think in terms of "Worst Case" scenarios. For example, when she was asked to pick a task that was not crucial to her job and then try to spend less energy and time on it, she decided to choose as her assignment a speech that was to be given to a high school class instead of to her peers. When she was asked to back off, to be less perfectionistic on this speech, therefore giving her more time to work on more important matters, at first she balked. It was almost impossible for her to think of giving a speech that was less than perfect or to ease up on the amount of time spent in preparation. I therefore asked her to think in "Worst Case" terms. "If you did present a speech that wasn't absolutely polished, what's the worst thing that could happen?" I asked. "Well, I don't know. I guess I'd be embarrassed." In front of teenagers? "Well some." What else? "They wouldn't ask me back." Would that be so bad? She laughed and said, "No, not really." When Marie began to think this way and ask herself, "OK, what *is* the worst thing that could happen?" she began to realize that usually even the worst things really weren't so bad.

What is important here is to begin to break the chain and to recognize that it's not the worry, anxiety, doubt, pain, and frenzied work that have made Impostors succeed. But change isn't always easy, especially when the patterns have existed for a long, long time and especially when the IP victim has the superstitious notion that he or she has to suffer in order to be successful. Trying to believe otherwise often can be frightening, too. But if you're a self-acknowledged Impostor and you do slowly begin to change, you'll probably find that no catastrophe occurs. In fact, you'll probably feel much safer and more secure as you change. With practice and with time, you'll learn how more realistically to appraise the amount of energy and work that are needed to be well prepared without being overprepared. And as this happens, you're likely to feel far less stress and finally more joy about your accomplishments.

TRUSTING PRAISE AND POSITIVE FEEDBACK

A critical element in removing the Impostor Mask and breaking the Impostor Cycle is to change the way evaluations and praise are received. As we noted in Chapters Three and Eight, IP victims are ingenious at negating or denying the objective evidence that they are indeed bright and successful.

Generally these people are not aware of this process, and just as it was crucial that they become conscious of the fact that they were wearing an Impostor Mask, it's also important that they realize and admit they're dismissing all proof that they're intelligent, creative, productive individuals. It's also important to remember that these people are absolutely sincere when they reject praise. The students I talked about in Chapter Eight, who made every possible excuse for their getting into an excellent university — including the one about the admissions committee making a mistake — were not being coy or flip. They truly believed there was no way they were smart enough or qualified enough to have gotten in on their own, and they honestly thought their being accepted must have been due to some error.

Some Impostors are so absolutely positive of their inability that if they were in a room surrounded by two hundred people, and 199 admired and praised them while only one person criticized, they would forget all the compliments and dwell on that one individual's negative response. Again, it's important to remember that these people are not giving a show of false modesty nor are they working on some ploy to gain that one extra person's approval. These Impostor sufferers simply are unable to hear all the outward praise and believe that it has anything to do with them. No matter what accolades are bestowed on them, no matter what the tangible evidence of their success, they sadly continue to foster the belief that they are not as good as everyone else. I say "sadly" because it is sad to see these very pleasant, deserving, intelligent people live with the notion that those who give them praise somehow must be wrong, or inept, or both.

The following experiment, if followed, may help IP victims begin to realize whether or not they are acting in such a way.

- In your notebook, keep a record for a week of any positive feedback or any compliments you receive. Next, note how you responded verbally and physically to the praise. After doing this, try to remember what you actually thought at the time, and write down that mental response. For example, in Timothy's notebook he wrote:

Fred said:	Response:	Mental Response:
"That was an excellent report you gave to the board."	"Thanks, the board is very responsive." Then I changed the subject.	I had a lot of help and I should have analyzed the cost factors.

In this instance, Timothy did say thanks, but he also subtly implied that his report was good only because the board normally was receptive. He quickly changed the subject and failed to ask Fred what he had liked about the report. Internally, he chastised himself for not doing all he could have done, and he focused on the one possible deficiency in his report.

~ ~ ~

Melissa wrote the following in her notebook after a test was returned with a grade of 97 and the comment, "Excellent work!" written on her paper.

Other Students said:	Response:	Mental Response:
"You really aced that one."	"I got lucky. I had a hunch about the kinds of questions she would ask."	I really didn't do so well on question 10. I forgot to put in an important reference. Sometimes I can be so dumb.

Melissa negated her teacher's comment and dismissed the compliments of her fellow students. She contributed her success to lucky intuition rather than her ability to know what was important, and she concentrated on what she didn't know rather than all the information she obviously knew well.

When I questioned her in therapy about her refusal to accept such positive feedback, she said, "I always concentrate more on my failures than my successes." I asked her what she might gain by doing that. "Well, I won't be so hurt by failure if I expect it."

"So you want to stay prepared for any possible failure."

"Yes, I'm afraid to let up. If I expect failure, maybe I can handle it." After this, we spent several sessions dealing with her terror of failure and her fear of admitting she was good.

~ ~ ~

THE IMPOSTOR PHENOMENON

Katherine received her annual review and her supervisor rated her at Level 5 (the highest rating) in five different areas of performance. In the sixth area, creativity, she was rated at Level 4 (very good). In her notebook, she recorded the following about this review.

Supervisor's Ratings:	Response:	Mental Response:
Highest level on five criteria. Next to the highest on creativity.	Temporary high feeling. I thanked him for his help.	At first I felt good, but not having all 5's began to bother me more and more. Kept thinking, "I can't make it if I'm not creative."

Katherine felt good temporarily but gave much more weight to the score that was lowest than to the five very high ones. She began to worry so much about it that she could not internalize the other parts of the evaluation, which, of course, were excellent.

~ ~ ~

John was another client who had great difficulty accepting praise and realizing *why* the praise was given. This man had started his own consulting business and often had to work with important clients. When he expressed his doubts in therapy, he asked, "What do I have to offer these people? I'm surprised that they come to me at all." When he followed the above exercise of writing down positive feedback and recognized how he discounted others' opinions, he realized aloud, "If I think I've fooled these people, then I'm saying that their opinions don't matter, and I'm saying that they're not very smart."

He began to see that if he valued their judgment, then their judgment about *him* must be right. "After all," he finally admitted, "one would have to be very bright to fool such important, intelligent people." It soon seemed much more realistic to John to accept their positive feedback.

- After you've entered the information in your notebook, notice any gimmicks you use to dismiss the praise or make it unimportant. Ask yourself, "What will happen if I accept the positive feedback as representing the truth?" Pause and see what responses come. Some people are afraid of becoming arrogant or complacent if they begin to believe the good things that are said about them. Others are afraid they will lose their motivation, and many are afraid that people will be jealous or dislike them. Try to determine if you're afraid of such things.

- Now decide that you will experiment with changing your behavior for one week. During this time, try accepting and receiving positive feedback; make no attempt to minimize or negate it. If you know someone else with IP doubts, you might team up with them and compare notes. See how you feel when you accept and believe the feedback. You may be surprised to find you are enjoying some of your successes more. You may also find that you are very resistant to trying this experiment and sticking with it. If you are resistant, see if there are advantages to dismissing the praise. Does your dismissal result in repeated efforts by others to convince you and persuade you that you are fine?

Recall your answers to the questions about your family and the messages you were taught. Since the feedback from your family and others probably was incongruent, you may be afraid of trusting feedback now. You still may be expecting discrepancies (in fact, you still may be *receiving* discrepancies as an adult, especially if your success is atypical for your family or if they are not totally supportive of what you do). If so, your resistance to changing in the here and now may be your wish to get the desired feedback from parents and siblings. If you believe that is what's happening, see if realizing it makes the experiment easier. Then complete the following sentence: "I'm having trouble changing this behavior of negating praise because . . ." If your reasons have something to do with your family, think about how accepting praise would affect your relationship with them. Imagine someone saying to you, "You did an excellent job on that new project. You should be awfully proud." Next imagine yourself replying, "Thank you. I am proud." Now imagine yourself believing it. And if you did, would it really affect the way your family looks at you? Would you lose their respect or their love?

If you're afraid you may become arrogant as a result of acknowledging such praise, remember that most Impostors are very sensitive, agreeable people. With a great deal of practice, they may be able to change their attitudes and their behavior; it's far less likely that their likable personalities will change.

13 | Overcoming IP Fears And Guilts

CAROL ANN AND Merry Pat were the two women we saw in Chapter Six who were terrified of failing. Both of these women were very bright and both obviously knew that most people who succeed also occasionally make mistakes or fail. But the idea of such a thing was intolerable to the two of them.

The first woman, Carol Ann, was mortified when she thought she had failed at giving a workshop for speech and drama teachers. Actually, we saw, the workshop participants had not appeared impressed with Carol Ann because they simply were not listening; they had been too self-absorbed and concerned with what people were thinking of them to pay attention. But this woman's opinion of her ability was so low that she thought there could be only one reason for their lack of adulation — she wasn't very good. Before her self-doubts could be removed, she first had to try and understand why she was so afraid of failing, and then try to overcome this fear.

The second young woman, Merry Pat, not only was afraid of failing but in a way actually did fail. She is the professor whose contract was not renewed at the college where she had been teaching. The unrenewed contract was unt to being fired in Merry Pat's mind, and it was a devastating blow.

With both of these women, after much discussion and therapy work, it was evident that they were afraid of failing for the same reason: they were afraid that if they failed, it would mean they were no longer liked or respected. Carol Ann was afraid her colleagues would think her inept and wouldn't have anything to do with her. Merry Pat believed all her years of education would have been wasted. And both women were afraid that if their parents and close friends found out about such failings, they would withdraw their love; and the thought of losing such love was more than either woman believed she could bear.

But once they realized they were afraid of failing, and once they understood why, there was hope that they could overcome their fears. And if they overcame their terror of failing, there was also great probability that their self-esteem would rise.

OVERCOMING THE FEAR OF FAILURE

Like Merry Pat and Carol Ann, most IP victims associate failure with humiliation and profound shame, and they avoid any behavior that might make them look foolish or dumb. It's therefore very important to modify this tendency, or the victims likely will never allow themselves to take appropriate risks and learn to act and react spontaneously. If you fall into this category, the following exercise may help:

- Take a moment and think back over your life. Try to remember any times when you felt humiliated or shamed because of a mistake you made or some embarrassing situation that was observed by others. Let yourself reexperience those times and the feelings you had. Probably you resolved then that you'd never allow yourself to feel so bad again; you made a promise to yourself that you'd stay on top of things. You were also probably very small and vulnerable when you experienced such shame. Therefore, imagine the same experience happening to you now that you are an adult, stronger and more successful. Fantasize that you are powerful enough to change the situation so that you do not feel ashamed. Visualize the experience with a more favorable outcome. See how you feel now.

As a result of the above exercise, Alan remembered vividly several instances in which he had felt shamed by his sister. He recalled a particular incident in which he had just completed a drawing of a man but had failed to give the man fingers and feet. The sister, who was six years older than Alan, had teased and laughed at him when she saw the drawing. He also remembered that she had taunted him when he couldn't tell time and that she had called him a "dummy." He had forgotten these humiliating experiences before following the exercise, but when he remembered them, he understood more clearly why he had a real terror of appearing inept in any way.

Debra recalled her early attempts to learn the alphabet as a child. Her mother was trying to teach her but would always get impatient and yell, "You'll never learn it! That's not right. Listen to me." When she was spoken to this way, Debra always started to cry, but instead of being soothing, her mother would say, "I can't teach you anything."

After one of these episodes, she overheard her mother explaining to a neighbor, "Debra is so sensitive. She takes everything I say so seriously. Johnny would never let me get to him that way." Debra soon began to feel that such incidents were her fault. She blamed herself, but she was still frightened each time she had to learn something from her mother. With great resolution, she decided, "I'll show her. I won't cry again." She was on guard not to show her feelings and not to make mistakes. She was afraid that if she did make some error, she could expect the same kind of angry, frustrated response from her mother.

- If you didn't personally have such an experience as a child, then search your memory to see if you can recall seeing one of your parents or a sibling or some other person who was close to you being shamed because of a mistake or inappropriate action.

In this recall experiment, another client, Charles, remembered an incident in which someone he loved was embarrassed. His mother was an immigrant who spoke only broken English. He remembered that once, when he accompanied her to a school meeting, she tried to ask a question but kept stumbling over her words and was unable to make herself understood. Some people in the back of the room had snickered at her, Charles painfully recalled. Because of this, his mother had blushed and seemed badly embarrassed, and after this she refused to return to the school again. Charles had felt genuinely sorry for her — vicariously experiencing her humiliation — but he was also ashamed of her at the same time. And although he was only eight years old, he made a resolution at that moment never to look foolish or to be shamed as his mother had. Later he forgot how and when he had made such a decision. He only knew that he was desperately afraid of making an error and of looking foolish, but until he conducted this experiment, he didn't know why.

Paula's fear of making mistakes came from observing what happened to her sister. Many times she had seen this older sibling being scolded or whipped by their father. The punishment could come from something as simple as spilling her milk at the dinner table to bringing home bad grades. Paula became so afraid of being treated this way herself that she became judicious and careful about everything she did. She also tried to become rather invisible, and she learned how to keep from standing out or having any attention drawn toward her. Even though as an adult she's no longer vulnerable to the moods and whims of someone so volatile as her father, she still acts cautiously and tries not to take up much space, as if she's still afraid a hand might reach out at any time and strike her. If she does make a mistake, she has an unconscious fear of being hurt and a conscious sense of panic. After remembering these family scenes and realizing why she carries such fears, she slowly is becoming able to work on them, and eventually she even may be able to manage them.

Jonathan had no such unpleasant memories about his family, but he did remember critical instances from the first grade. His teacher that year was the kind of person who made derogatory remarks when the children had trouble reading or when they made mistakes. She put stars by the names of the good students and red X's by the names of those who were having trouble. And if the children laughed at someone who made an error, she didn't stop them but seemed to encourage the teasing and the laughter. Jonathan decided then, as a six-year-old, that no one would ever be given a chance to laugh at him and that he'd be so careful he would never fail. As a man in his thirties, he's still trying to stick to those vows.

All of these memories indicate the kind of early experience that may contribute to developing a terror of failure. Most IP victims have had similar incidents in their lives, or they've had families who valued excellence to the extent that they felt much was expected of them. Obviously, most of us want to avoid failing. Yet the reality is that when people are reaching toward accomplishments, they're likely to make some mistakes along the way or even occasionally fail. Therefore, as a coping exercise, begin trying to say to yourself, "If I make a mistake or fail in some aspect of my work or my life, I can and will live through it. A failure will not devastate or destroy me. It's how I cope with mistakes or failures that ultimately matters." And if you do make mistakes, try not to berate or hate yourself. Instead, try to nurture your mind and body, and give yourself the message that you can keep on going. And instead of feeling trapped and defeated by a mistake, take some time to do all you can to convert the failure to success.

In his autobiography, automobile executive Lee Iacocca demonstrates how one can turn around failure and make it become a triumph. When he was fired from one of the top positions at the Ford Motor Company, it could have been a devastating time in his life. Instead, Iacocca kept pushing. He is now President of Chrysler Motor Company and is one of the most respected, successful businessmen in the country.

That kind of perseverance does not always come easily. But over the years many of my clients have realized that their fear of possible failure was worse than dealing with an actual crisis. They've found that they can handle firings, demotions, and other rejections and often in creative ways. Instead of saying, "I could never live through such an experience," they've begun to think, "I can live with and cope with any mistake I make or any failure that comes my way."

CHANGING PERFECTIONISM

If you are in the throes of perfectionism, it's more than likely that you will get anxious as you think about a change. The important thing to remember is that talking about change does not mean talking about lowering standards. Mediocrity is not being advocated here! Becoming more selective about your perfectionism and setting priorities *is* being advocated.

To begin to do so, it may be helpful for you to analyze your daily activities and determine how much time you spend on each one. Are there some activities which really aren't as important as others and could be handled more quickly and with less energy? If so, pick one of those activities or a particular project at work and decide to do it adequately and sufficiently rather than perfectly. If you select carefully, the change will not be noticed by others, but chances are it will relieve some of the pressure that's been on you. Again, remember that it's fine for you to maintain your standards of excellence in the important aspects of your job and your life. The key is to determine where those high standards are really needed.

ROSALYN

Rosalyn is a librarian who is in charge of a large department within a large metropolitan library. This IP victim believed all her work had to be absolutely perfect, but she began finding it more and more difficult to meet her standards as her department grew and the professional demands on her also increased. In therapy she was taught to discriminate between those items that needed her best efforts and those which did not. For example, it was important that she do an excellent job on her annual budget projections; here her high standards were helpful and definitely paid off. But when matters such as sending out departmental memorandums on minor policy changes came up, she realized her work did not have to be outstanding. It was unnecessary for her to proof such material three or four times or rewrite it still once more before distributing it to personnel. When she learned to make such separations in her mind, she found she was left with more time to enjoy her life and do a more thorough job on those things which truly required excellence.

Before she made these changes, though, Rosalyn needed to look at her perfectionism and determine how and why she had come to value it so. Her underlying fear was, "If I'm not perfect, I won't be loved or respected." In her thinking, a person was loved because of what they did and how well they did it. She couldn't even fathom the idea that someone might be loved for themselves and not for their productivity.

Her role model for such beliefs was a very powerful mother. In Rosalyn's eyes, her mother *was* perfect. This woman was successful in her business and had been promoted rapidly. She was also an excellent cook and a wonderful seamstress. In her beautiful clothes, she was always at the height of fashion. She also had a flair for decorating, and her home was as well dressed as she. But at the same time, she could handle practical matters such as minor plumbing problems, maintenance of the family car, and she could care for a sick child. It seemed that her mother knew just about everything, and Rosalyn felt she could never match such perfection.

But as Rosalyn began talking about her mother, she realized that the woman had never taken the time to teach her daughter how to do all the things she did so well. Or if she did try to teach, she became impatient and easily irritated if Rosalyn couldn't learn something right away. Rosalyn remembered a particular incident when her mother decided to teach her to sew. The pattern for a dress was laid out, the fabric cut, and the pieces pinned together. But as Rosalyn took a seat in front of the sewing machine, her mother immediately lost patience when she thought Rosalyn was too slow, or when she had difficulty replacing an empty bobbin, or when she put in a crooked, poorly executed seam. The more her mother criticized, the more nervous Rosalyn became. The scene finally ended with her mother taking over, claiming she would just do it herself, and with Rosalyn retreating to her room, angry, hurt, and fearful she could never do anything well.

Because of such incidents, she often felt stupid and believed that she should be able to do such things without being taught. After all, who had taught her mother? *She* seemed to know how to do everything instinctively. Rosalyn's mother was a powerful, competent woman, but it's very unlikely she was perfect or even knew how to do everything well. But in Rosalyn's mind, it was difficult to think of her mother in any other way, and she therefore had to deal with her need to be like this woman. She also discussed her belief that her mother would love her only if she were perfect, and that others in her life would react the same way.

Over a period of time, Rosalyn recognized that she didn't have to be a superwoman in order to be loved and respected. She also began to realize that her strengths were different from those of her mother. For example, she was much better at intellectual pursuits and in developing satisfying relationships. After a while, she also began to admit that she wanted more joy and less work in her life than her mother had found.

● If you have perfectionistic tendencies that you want to change, ask yourself the following question: "What will happen if I do not do this perfectly?" See if you can discover what your catastrophic expectations are, and then decide if they are really likely to come true.

Next, see if you can remember who was the role model for your perfectionism. Did a parent have such a disposition? An aunt or uncle? An influential teacher? An older sibling? If you did have such a role model, and you determine who that person is, ask yourself whether or not you want to repeat the patterns of that individual. Is it possible that this particular person, in spite of his or her high standards, really hasn't had such a satisfying life?

If you decide that you don't want to follow such patterns, then practice the exercise described at the beginning of this section. Be patient with yourself if change is difficult. You developed this characteristic over many years, so don't expect it to be undone quickly. At first it may be very tough for you to ease up and expect less of yourself, even on the most insignificant jobs. But if you practice and give yourself time, you can make regular, reliable change. And you will have more time to do your best work on those projects that require excellence.

THE PERFECTIONISTIC MOTHER

In Chapter Seven we discussed how Impostor fears seem to occur more acutely than ever when IP victims enter motherhood. It's a joyful yet highly stressful time, when the new mother feels pulled in many directions and is constantly afraid she will be less than perfect in caring for her child. Although many of these women feel isolated, depressed, and begin to wonder if maybe they're going crazy, most of them are simply overworked.

When I worked with many mothers at the family and child guidance clinic, it was obvious that nearly every one of them needed help with child care and with their household work. They also needed time for their own self-development. In therapy, we worked together to get these women to not feel guilty because they needed help; we also worked at getting them to accept the fact that, like their children and their partners, they had needs too.

When possible, we actively worked with their partners, urging them to take greater roles in parenting and to handle or assist with more of the domestic tasks. And I actively worked with the mothers to help them locate competent child care. To find such care, we called local churches and asked the ministers for the names of women whose children were grown but who might enjoy baby-sitting. We also called the psychology and nursing departments of local colleges and asked for the names of competent students, who might want to provide the same kind of services. These mothers were so overwhelmed that they felt unable to do this calling alone; therefore we made such inquiries together. And when we finished, we were able to compile a list of reliable, concerned baby sitters who had good references.

We also discovered that several local libraries provided storytelling sessions once a week for children three years of age and older. With such sessions available, the mothers were able to take their children to the library for two or three hours a week, and they were free to browse through the library themselves, to run errands, or to do whatever they needed or wanted to do with their time. We found several churches and synagogues, too, that provided good supervised child care and interesting programs for the children. Again, such services provided these women with the time they so desperately needed; and with some relief from the responsibilities of their children, their fatigue and distress were decreased considerably.

Sometimes while I was urging the women to obtain adequate child care, they told me that they couldn't afford such help. Yet the irony of this was that if a psychiatrist wrote a prescription for them for an antidepressant, none of them ever complained that she didn't have the money to fill the prescription. It became apparent that it was harder for them to justify using money for household and child care assistance (because they believed they should be able to do it all themselves) than it was to take an antidepressant drug. We therefore had to spend considerable time talking about their qualms for getting such help and spending money on themselves.

For mothers who were working part-time or full-time, the question of finding quality care was even tougher. However, ministers, rabbis, social workers, psychologists, and local colleges were still excellent resources for finding the names of good people or good centers that could provide high-caliber care. In taking an active role in this process, I realized more than ever the critical need for good child care in this country.

Some of the women I worked with also decided to cooperate with one another in the hiring of a very competent individual who would care for five or six children at a time. By working together, these mothers were able to pay better wages and hire a more qualified person to not only baby-sit but also teach their children. Such a joint venture alleviated some of the financial burden from each family. They were able to afford more quality care for their children for less money.

- If you're a mother (or father) who feels overwhelmed by the responsibilities of parenting, try to remember this is not only a very joyful time but also a very stressful one. If you're feeling guilty about how overwhelmed you are and feel that you should be able to do it all, try to remember how your mother or father handled similar situations. Chances are they had more help than you first remembered. Was there a relative who was able to pitch in occasionally, or a friend or neighbor?

Now try to think about the time you are spending with your child. Are you anxious part of the time? Do you feel tired, overworked, or depressed? If so, do you think these feelings are being passed on to your child? Do you think the baby might be picking up on how stressed you are? If so, think about how it might be better for both of you if you were able to have some time away from the child. Would you actually be a better parent if you had an hour or two to yourself once or twice a week?

If you feel any of these things, try to remember that you're not alone. Also tell yourself that it's OK to need help and then to find that help.

Local churches, synagogues, colleges, and libraries are excellent sources for finding assistance. Even if your church does not provide mother's-day-out programs, your minister or rabbi still may be able to put you in touch with individuals who might be willing to baby-sit at least on a part-time basis. If you're still having difficulty finding adequate care, seek out other mothers in your neighborhood or town who might be having the same problems, and then see if you can't find help together. If nothing else, the support of other mothers probably will prove helpful to you.

DEALING WITH THE NEED TO BE
THE VERY BEST

As we saw earlier in the book, many IP victims not only have to feel they're perfect, they also believe they have to be more perfect than anyone else. This need can be particularly debilitating, because in many work settings a number of people are outstanding and special. If one has to be the star to feel worthwhile, then that need is seldom going to be satisfied.

- If you recognize this symptom in yourself, make an assessment as to whether or not you're squelching your own development by avoiding tough, risk-taking situations. Are you avoiding promotion or advancement or new endeavors because you're only one of many competent people in such a situation? If so, think about the risks that would be involved in making the different moves.

Think about yourself and your present level of functioning. In what ways are you special and outstanding? In what ways are you very competent but also very similar to others around you? What would happen if you stopped being so afraid of not being the very best?

HENRY

There's no doubt that in almost everything this man had ever tried, he was outstanding. But after receiving his MBA and joining a very prestigious accounting firm, he almost immediately became panicky and began suffering from anxiety attacks. He longed to be the very best accountant and to be the one most respected by the senior officers in the firm. He received feedback indicating that these people liked and respected him and that they thought he would do well, but there was no indication that Henry was the firm's star. In fact, the company had no stars. It employed so many bright and capable people that nearly all of them received recognition at different times.

But since Henry wasn't considered the best, he began to fear he also wasn't as good as the others, and he began to worry about all of the information he believed he didn't know. In our therapy work, he became consciously aware of his need to be the star, and he worked with his feelings of envy and jealousy. Slowly he came to realize that it was possible for him to be very competent and outstanding and even among the top one percent of the national population in intellectual ability, while the other people in his firm probably also were among the top one percent in the country. Yet even though he was surrounded by other such intelligent individuals, it was important for him to admit that he did have his own special gifts. Just because others were bright didn't mean he suddenly became less so, he learned.

Part of our therapy concerned having Henry do volunteer work in other organizations, where he was able to experience how very special he was and where he received considerable recognition for his abilities. He also had to work with his competitive and sometimes jealous feelings. Part of the therapy here dealt with simply recognizing when these feelings arose and why. Once he understood such tendencies, he was able to realize that both he and his co-workers could do brilliant work, that all of them were special in unique ways, and that there was enough recognition to be distributed among the entire staff.

There is one other element that is important in understanding Henry and the way he perceived himself. His family had always communicated to him that he was to excel and become successful. But they also let him know that the path he had taken, in becoming an accountant, was not what they had expected. They believed Henry had so much potential that they were disappointed when he didn't become someone famous — an actor, possibly, or a well-known surgeon. They let him know that being an accountant seemed a comparatively unimportant profession, and that even though he had joined a prestigious firm and his chances for advancement were good, it wasn't good enough for him. In therapy, Henry became more aware of his fear that he had failed his family. He also realized, gradually, that what he wanted for his life might be different from what his family had wanted, but that didn't make it any less important. When he began to accept these

things, he came closer to losing his fears and haɑ ʟ̶
feelings of being an Impostor.

OVERCOMING FEAR OF AND
GUILT ABOUT SUCCESS

Andrew Young, America's former United Nations
ambassador and now mayor of Atlanta, recently gave a
poignant and wise account of what it can be like to feel
guilty about success. In a speech, Young described a famil-
iar American scene where the family is sitting down to
Thanksgiving dinner. But before the family can begin their
meal, the wife says how sad it is to think about the starving
children in Ethiopia, especially when she and her family
have so much. Andrew Young is far from being an insen-
sitive, uncaring man, but when his wife made this remark,
he said he didn't want to have to think about and feel guilty
about the starving children of Africa while he ate his
Thanksgiving turkey.

Young went on to explain that he doesn't think it is
always helpful or productive to feel guilty about the things
one has. "You don't make people more responsible by
making them feel guilty," he said. Instead of feeling guilty,
he stressed, it's important to use one's power, and intelligence, and money and to be active in changing policies
and providing opportunities for people who do not have as
much. I think Young's points are important ones; people
can be empathetic of others' needs and benevolent towards
the less fortunate, but at the same time they don't necessarily have to give up all they've worked for in order to feel
that they are helping. Young's address helps us all to
remember that guilt doesn't have to accompany success.

Yet many of my clients struggle with the issue of having

more success, more education, or more financial rewards than other members of their family or the community in which they were reared; and many others feel the same kind of guilt because they've come from exceptionally successful families where they've received far more advantages than most people around them. These people generally are very sensitive, caring individuals who experience pain and guilt because so many around them do not have the amenities they have or the opportunities to succeed. This guilt often prevents them from being happy about what they have. And out of guilt, they quickly slip into Impostor-like behaviors and say to themselves, "I'm not really this bright, and I haven't really been very successful." They acknowledge that luck, having the right contacts, attending the right schools, and being pleasant or charming played important roles in their success.

It's true that such factors help people to get ahead, but it's also true that others with the same advantages haven't succeeded nearly so well. It's important for IP victims to realize that even though they may have been helped along the way and had many advantages, they also probably could not have gone so far if they hadn't been capable individuals. They need to remember that there are indeed many bright people who haven't succeeded because they didn't have advantages; but they also need to remember that guilt alone cannot undo the injustices of the world, and IP-caused guilt will not help other people succeed.

- If you're having difficulty enjoying your success without feeling guilty, start trying to change your guilt by rereading and acknowledging the above statements. Then say to yourself, "It is true that some part of my success may be due to luck, to hard work, to knowing the right people, or to having the opportunities that my family provided, but it is also true that it takes intelligence to utilize such luck and opportunities. And I have been bright enough to use the gifts I have received."

Now, say to yourself, "There are many inherently bright people who have not been able to succeed because they haven't had the advantages and they haven't had the right opportunities." Think about this statement for a minute, then ask yourself the following question: "How does my feeling guilty help?" It's likely that your answer will be, "It doesn't."

Next, ask yourself, "What would help others more than my feeling guilty? What can I do?"

One of my clients who was feeling guilty about being more successful than her sister went through the above exercise. After asking herself these questions, she realized her guilt was helping no one. But she realized that positive action would. She therefore set up a trust fund for the education of her sister's children. She now puts a hundred dollars a month in the fund, and by the time her nieces and nephew reach college age, the fund will help substantially.

Another client, an attorney who was experiencing the same kind of IP-induced guilt, now sees ten percent of his clients at a very reduced rate or for no fee at all. These clients are individuals who would not be able to afford good legal counseling otherwise. This man sticks to the ten percent, allowing himself to do well financially, but because he is greatly helping clients, he feels less guilty and is able to let go of some of his IP feelings.

One young woman who was experiencing tremendous

guilt about her success now gives two days a month from her regular job to tutor children in reading. She knows that teaching the disadvantaged to read is one of the first steps in opening doors for them. This woman took positive, concrete steps in doing something to assist in the many needs she saw all around her instead of sitting at home and staying wrapped forever in her guilt.

Another client now sits on an advisory board for a large business, and he constantly monitors whether or not this company and its board make important community contributions. Again, like the others mentioned, because he is taking action rather than hiding behind an Impostor Mask and saying, "I'm not successful" to alleviate his guilt, he is able to enjoy his success.

Each person has to work out his or her own plan of action — one that fits their needs or interests. But finding a way to be generous with one's time or talents or money is an effective, positive way to deal with guilt about success.

MYTHS ABOUT SUCCESS

Another way to overcome the fear of and guilt about doing well is to recognize some of the hidden myths or misconceptions you may have about success. For most people, until they become aware of their deepest feelings about success, it's difficult for them to remove their fear of getting ahead. The following exercise can help you to understand such feelings and possible myths.

- Imagine that you are very successful and that you are publicly recognized by others in your field as being so. Now see yourself in that role. What do you look like? How do you feel? Now fantasize having a brief conversation with the following people about your success. In the conversation, what would these individuals say?

Your father.	(If your parents are not living,
Your mother.	still imagine the conversation as
	if they were living.)

Your siblings.
Your partner, spouse, or lover.
One or two colleagues.
A good friend.
A favorite teacher or a mentor.

The results of this exercise are very varied for each individual, but chances are that the imaginary conversations will be accompanied by powerful feelings. One woman musician, in her fantasized conversation with her lover, recognized that he would be threatened if she became more successful than he. She then realized that she had been passing up opportunities because she was afraid of his reaction. She was also afraid that if she became very successful, she might lose him. After this exercise, she knew she needed to talk with him and see if there were ways they could work it out. She realized, too, that she might have to risk losing him in order to stop being afraid. He might not be able to tolerate her being as successful as she could be, but she was no longer willing to squelch her creativity.

When a minister tried this exercise, he heard his parents telling him to "be humble in mind, body, and spirit." He believed that to do so he needed to stay poor. And in the past, in order to please them, he had stayed in small parishes even though he had wanted to move to a city church. As he talked, he realized that they were afraid of losing his time and his interest if he moved away. This exercise helped him to realize that he had to choose between living his life the way his parents wanted it or the way he wanted it.

A male biologist recognized that he and his brother were very competitive. They both had a tendency to want to be the best, and both were still competing for their father's love even though they were in their forties. When he followed this exercise, the biologist also realized that his brother always pleased their father more. This was due in part, he believed, to his brother's following in the older man's path and becoming a businessman. During family get-togethers, his dad often changed the conversation from what the biologist son was doing to what the brother was doing. When he realized these truths, he was saddened, but he also realized that he had tried to replace his father's attention with someone else's. Since he felt he could not be special in his father's eyes, he had tried to be the very best or the most special in the eyes of his boss. And although it might not be the same as pleasing his father, he knew that he had earned the respect of someone who meant a great deal to him.

In imagined conversations with her mother and father, a young nurse recognized that her parents had always believed in her very strongly. They were supportive and caring, but as she worked her way through the fantasized dialogue with them, she realized that she had failed to acknowledge their support.

Ellen's reaction to this fantasy was equally revealing. Her father was indifferent to her success, but in the imagined conversation with her mother she was told, "You're going to be killed in a plane crash if you keep going out to give all of these speeches." Ellen then had an "Aha!" kind of experience. Whenever her career had taken a definite step forward, she had always become very anxious. In fact, at times, she felt sheer panic. But while discussing this fantasy exercise, she realized that at some level she had bought her mother's superstition. This parent's message had been — "If you're too successful, something bad will happen. You may even die." As a result of this conversation with her mother, she was able to recognize what was happening to her when she felt panic. She was able to say, "I'm afraid something bad will happen because I've taken another step toward success." Knowing the source of her fear and clearly noting that it was a superstitious, irrational fear helped her to overcome her panic about succeeding.

After recognizing the role her family played in creating her IP feelings, Ellen spent considerable time in her therapy expressing her anger at them. Then she realized that she also felt hurt and disappointment beneath the anger. After much work, she began to try to understand what had made her mother so frightened of success. And she was able to trace her mother's attitudes to her own upbringing, thus understanding them more; when this happened, much of her anger, along with her own fears, began to disappear.

- As you recall your own fantasy about success and the reactions of the important people in your life, see if you can summarize the messages you are receiving about success. Are you being supported, or are you being told to be careful? Are some people threatened by or scared of your possible success? Are you afraid of losing their love or acceptance if you fully use your abilities?

If you have felt scared when you've made advances in your career, these fantasy exercises may help you to understand the source of your fears. If you know the source, you can cope better with the fears and learn to change them.

- Sometimes Impostors cannot even fantasize themselves as being successful. They draw a blank and can't come up with images at all. If you fall into this category, it's likely that you have a real fear of success. Notice the dreams you have at night, and see if these dreams portray you as being frightened.

  If so, when you're with a group of trusted friends, ask them to do the fantasy experiment with you. Listen to their responses. As you do this, you may be able to fantasize also. If not, don't push yourself. It's likely that a spontaneous fantasy will come to you at a later time when you are not deliberately trying so hard.

As you try these exercises and begin to truly understand how you and others feel about your success, you may decide you can live without the love of someone who is unable to accept who you are. Often, however, others can change and deal with their concerns as you change, especially if you're willing to talk with them and let them know that you will not be altering how much you care for them just because you're becoming more successful.

The other discovery that is often made during these fantasy experiments is that people are afraid that if they become more successful, or if they recognize their success, they might have to take on more duties and more responsibilities. The person may feel they're already functioning at their limit. But if they maintain their Impostor feelings, they can think and say, "I can't do it. I can't handle this." In a way, then, Impostor feelings protect them from taking on more, and it's a way for them not to have to admit that they want more joy and less work in their lives. In order to change "I can't" to "I don't want to," these people need to be taught how to say no and how to ask for help.

14 | Learning To Enjoy Success

A S WE MENTIONED in the previous chapter, one
reason so many IP victims fear success is because they
believe it will bring on added responsibilities and even
more work. Most of these people feel they're already pro-
ducing as much as they possibly can. Therefore, the idea of
having to produce more or having even more demands
made of their time and their energy is more than they think
they can stand. "I can't handle anymore," is one of the
statements I hear often.

IP victims say such things not because they don't want to
be successful, but because they want more joy and less work
in their lives. They've probably seen others — parents or
employers, possibly — who are very successful but never
have time to enjoy what they've earned. These people have
decided this is not the way they want to live. But instead of
fearing success and staying in lower positions because they
don't want to be constantly overworked, they need to find
more positive ways to deal with the problem.

LEARNING TO GET HELP

Jim and Joan were a two-career couple who were

advancing rapidly in their careers. He was a dentist, she was a sociologist, and they both were feeling over-whelmed.

First of all, they were having trouble managing their house, chauffeuring the children, and attending all their professional functions. Joan felt responsible for most of the first two items, and she was upset that Jim wasn't helping more. Even though this couple made a good deal of money, both partners resisted getting household help. Jim had exceedingly high standards and felt he must be like his father, who had always handled everything himself — including repair work around the house, driving the kids to basketball games, cooking occasionally, and numerous other things that Jim hardly ever had time for.

What Jim failed to recognize was that his father had had a much less demanding job than either he or Joan, and consequently had put in far fewer hours at work. In comparison, Jim worked long hours and was active in the local and national dental associations. And Joan felt the need to be a superwoman in all aspects of her life. She demanded beauty, intelligence, charm, and creativity of herself at all times.

With so many expectations of themselves, this couple was experiencing tremendous stress, burnout, and Impostor feelings. They therefore were experiencing little joy in their relationship, and they came to me for help.

It didn't take me long to see that part of their problem was simply a lack of time for intimacy. I quickly started working with them to obtain hired help for many of their home projects. Even though they had the money for such help, they were highly resistant to seeking it in the begin-ning. They continued to believe that they should be able to do everything themselves. But after much coaching, they consented to get a cleaning service twice a week, hire caterers whenever they gave a party, take their clothes to a laundry, and hire a clinical child psychology graduate student to pick up their children after school and to stay with them until either Jim or Joan got home. Because the graduate student was capable, knowledgeable, and kind, they knew their children were being well taken care of and being taught new things. And when this couple did get home in the evenings, they finally had the energy and the inclination to prepare dinner together and enjoy a meal with their children.

Getting consistent, reliable help decreased their anxiety tremendously. And both became less afraid of success, because they knew that if they did become more successful, they could get adequate support to help them.

Before taking such action, they were constantly fighting about who should pick up the children, who should clean the house, who should do the shopping. Although getting assistance in these areas is not a panacea for marital problems, it does ease some of the tension and provide time for a couple such as Jim and Joan to talk and spend more hours of each day with one another. In their case, the children were also pleased that their parents seemed happier together and were arguing less. And both Jim and Joan became more efficient at setting priorities and began to recognize that their time was as valuable as their money. When they received invitations to parties or dinners with associates and friends, they began to take the time to really discuss whether or not they wanted to accept. They decided while in therapy never to answer such an invitation immediately, but to say that they must consult their calendar first and that they would get back to the person calling.

This technique provided them with the time to decide

how important an invitation was to each of them and why they would or would not accept it. Using this process they discovered that they had been going places and doing things with certain individuals simply to please the other.

The next thing we did in therapy was to have both of them rate, on a scale of one to ten, how important it was for one of them to do something with the other. For example, if Jim wanted to attend a sports event and Joan didn't very much want to go, she would ask him, using the one to ten scale, how important it was for her to accompany him. If his answer was an eight or a nine, then Joan would go; but if he didn't really care and answered with a two or a three, then Joan knew it was fine for her to do something else with her time. Using such a technique, they realized that both of them didn't always have to accept an invitation and that both of them didn't have to attend.

Joan was more of an extrovert than her husband, and she enjoyed parties far more than he did and usually wanted to stay much longer. Jim generally preferred to stay home. But when they started being more honest about what each wanted to do, they learned that they could take separate cars to such functions. If Jim chose to leave early and it didn't deeply matter to Joan whether or not he stayed, then he knew he could leave without either of them feeling guilty or angry.

As a result of their deliberate efforts to save time by hiring help whenever possible and setting new priorities, this couple had more time for their career developments and more quality time to spend together in sheer enjoyment. With less pressure on them, they began to do the things that had attracted them to each other initially. They began to spend time before falling asleep discussing their day or talking about politics — a favorite subject that they hadn't had time for in years. They began listening to music again and reading passages to one another from whatever book they were reading. As they played more, they had more energy and became interested in each other all over again. And as their interest improved, their lovemaking became more intense.

Although this couple made it a point to find more time for pleasure in their lives, they also made it a point to continue striving for excellence in their careers. They found that by setting priorities and finding reliable, competent help, they could have both. And as they did, they experienced a definite decrease in their IP feelings.

The techniques that Jim and Joan employed are ones that you can use if you are being overworked and feeling stress rather than joy as a result of your success. The first rule is to hire help when it is possible. By figuring out how much you are paid per hour, you'll probably find that it is cost effective to hire someone who is paid less to handle some of your responsibilities and tasks. The initial hiring may take time, but if you select carefully, you can find people who require little or no supervision. Often colleagues and friends can make referrals, and as I said in the previous chapter, churches and colleges are excellent sources for such help. But no matter where or how you get help, the key is to seek it when it's needed and not to feel guilty for having such a need.

That sounds like such a simple, obvious statement; yet in my fifteen years of doing therapy work, I have found that most people — especially Impostor sufferers — initially are very resistant to this idea. When my clients and I first explore the resistance, they essentially say, "I shouldn't hire anyone to do something I know how to do." And even when they are told, and agree, that it seems they don't have the time or energy to do such work, they still believe that it is wasteful to hire help. There usually is some underlying notion that if they're good enough, they should be able to do it themselves; and often such feelings come from comparing themselves to a parent who never had paid help.

- If you are resistant to getting help, think about why you are. Now try to remove the resistance and decide that you're going to take the risk of getting help, even if it may make you feel wasteful at first. Now take a look at your budget and financial resources, and determine how much help you can afford.

  Decide which of your duties are most time consuming and difficult for you, and decide that this is where you will spend your money getting help.

The second major complaint that most Impostors have in regard to paid services is that the work is not always done perfectly or exactly the way the IP victim wants it. In this case, it may be necessary to hire several people before you find the one who is satisfactory. But in the end, you also may have to change your expectations: there may not be anyone whose work will be as perfect as yours or who will absolutely please you. But if they are able to free you from some of your responsibilities, their imperfection may be a price that is worth paying.

LEARNING TO SAY NO

Millie Kagan, a social worker and therapist with many years of experience, taught me a tremendous lesson when she said, "Agencies will take as much as you will give."

THE IMPOSTOR PHENOMENON

Somehow I had developed the idealistic notion that people in authority could see when I had assumed my share of the committee work or when I had taken on too much, and they would not ask me to do more. But Millie's comment helped me to learn that other people will keep giving you work as long as you accept it. After learning this principle, I understood how important it is for people to become more active in deciding which new responsibilities they will add and which they will not. And when people become clearer about their limits, they generally are respected more.

But just as IP victims are resistant in getting help, they usually are resistant in learning to say no, too. Most are afraid that it will make them appear inadequate, and they begin to question their worth or ability if they can't take on more.

- If you have trouble saying no, see if you can understand why. Are you afraid you will not be liked or respected if you don't always say yes? Are you afraid you can make it only if you overwork? Are you afraid that someone else may take on the project you refuse and then get the credit?

Take a look at your attitudes toward taking on work. Recall your family messages regarding such things. Was hard work praised in your family? Were you given a label such as "lazy" that you are trying to overcome? See what you may need to change about those messages and begin the process.

Although hard work and success often go together,

highly successful people usually are very skilled at delegating tasks and at setting priorities and knowing what they need most to do. Therefore, the next time you are asked to take on a new activity or responsibility, take the time to decide whether or not you want to do it. Avoid the IP response of "I can't do it," which may be a cover for "I don't want to do it." If you have trouble deciding what to do, here are some important questions to ask:

How important is it that I do this?

What is likely to happen if I don't?

What will I have to give up if I accept it?

Do I really have the time to take it on?

If not, is there something else I can drop?

What will happen if I accept the responsibility and delegate much of the work?

If you take the time to answer these questions, you'll have a clearer idea of whether you want to say yes or no and some of the possible consequences of either answer.

Cynthia was a high school teacher who was loved and respected by her students and her peers. As a result of her high-quality work, she was asked to be advisor to many clubs, to represent her school at state activities, to hold office in the National Education Association, and to teach important classes. As she took on more and more responsibilities, she found herself feeling overwhelmed and began having strong IP experiences. She became very anxious and began to say, "I can't handle this."

When Cynthia was asked to examine her doubts, it became clear that she did not want to take on more activities. I encouraged her to go to her principal and explain that because of her many job-related responsibililties, her teaching load was too heavy; it was necessary for her to either lighten the load or give up some of the other activities. To her surprise, he was very willing to have someone else take one of her courses.

She began to understand there was a difference between not *wanting* to do something and not being able to do something. She experimented with saying, "I'd prefer not to take that on." Of course, she knew there would always be things she had to do which she didn't want to do, but she also discovered that she had far more power than she ever believed. Cynthia also learned that people often would continue to give her responsibilities as long as she would accept them, and that it was up to her to set reasonable limits for herself. As a result, she was able to do more of what she did superbly — teach.

- If you recognize that you have the tendency to take on more and more — to the point that you feel overwhelmed and often use Impostor excuses ("I'm not good enough, so I can't do that!") — think of when and where you could say, "No, I don't *want* to do that," instead. See what happens when you respond in such a way. Chances are that you'll find you're respected more by setting such limits rather than accepting any task that is given to you.

ENJOYING SUCCESS

You will know that you have succeeded in changing your IP profile if you are finding that you are able to acknowledge and accept your accomplishments and beginning to enjoy what you've accomplished. You may even find yourself willing to talk about a recent success in a more open, relaxed manner.

You're probably also becoming more realistic about your abilities, and even though you still might love to be considered a genius, you also realize that if you're not, it doesn't mean that you are stupid or inept. You may be in a setting where you are surrounded by many bright, special people, but hopefully you are beginning to realize that their existence doesn't mean you can't be bright and special too. Possibly you're beginning to realize that it's OK for you to have deficiencies in your knowledge, and you're beginning to acknowledge the many things you do know. And hopefully you're being more realistic about yourself and others — no longer overestimating their talents and underestimating yours.

I hope you're beginning to learn that the person who has been hiding beneath that Impostor Mask is a capable, intelligent person who more than likely will continue to succeed. And I hope that you can enjoy your success without the doubt, anxiety, and misery that have accompanied you for so long.

If, however, you can't make these changes on your own, it's important for you to remember than you can get assistance. For many years people were frightened or embarrassed to seek psychological help because they thought it meant they had a sickness or an abnormality. Fortunately that attitude is changing, and as more and more famous individuals such as Betty Ford openly indicate that they need help with problems, that stigma is fading.

Many companies and corporations are beginning to develop employee assistance programs that provide referral services or counseling. And some large firms are hiring consultants to provide workshops on issues such as stress management and burnout. Also psychologists, psychiatrists, social workers, ministers, rabbis, and counselors are providing more and more seminars that help people cope with life more effectively.

If you need assistance in overcoming your IP fears, I recommend that you try to find the workshops offered by these people and by local churches, colleges, and universities. Many also offer continuing education courses on developing self-esteem or dealing with success. If you're interested in individual help, you can call the psychological association or psychiatric association in your state for referrals. Or if you know someone who has received therapy and is pleased with its results, ask them for the name of the psychotherapist or counselor they saw. When change can't be achieved alone, these people may be able to provide you with help and improve the quality of your life tremendously.

But no matter how you seek help, if you have intense IP feelings, I hope you will work toward removing your fear of failure and your guilt about success; ease some of the demands you make of yourself; try becoming less perfectionistic all of the time; and learn to slowly accept the genuine praise of others. And as you do, I hope you'll remember this quote by W. Somerset Maugham: "Only a mediocre person is always at his best."

15

Working With IP Victims For Change

IF YOU LIVE with or love an Impostor or have an IP victim as a friend or colleague, you probably recognized them right away when you read about the components of the Impostor Profile. You probably can see clearly, too, the pain and frustration this person experiences, although you may not be able to understand it very well.

You probably have seen this intelligent individual succeed over and over again, and then you've watched him or her dismiss that success and reject your praise. And even if you're a very tolerant person, chances are that you've become frustrated yourself and have begun asking the questions, "Why can't such a bright, competent person learn that she is good?" "Why can't he believe me when I tell him how fantastic he is?"

If all your efforts to encourage the person and all your reassurances that he or she will be fine continue to fail, you probably have begun to feel helpless and no longer know what to do. If you have become the "Sympatheic Other" or "Frustrated Other" in such a relationship, the following suggestions may be helpful in your future conversations with adult IP victims. (Methods for helping younger victims will be covered in the next section of this chapter, ng Impostor-Free Children.")

DON'T:

- Ignore their fear and doubts.

- Rush to immediately reassure Impostors by saying such things as, "You've always done well in the past, and you'll do fine now."

- Tease them about their fears.

DO:

- Take their doubts and fears seriously.

- Encourage victims to talk more about what scares them. Instead of telling the victims that they always do well, ask them, "What makes you afraid this time?"

- Listen to their answers.

- Ask, "Do you mean that?" and see if you can understand their concerns.

- Ask yourself whether or not you have heard the feelings — the fear, the doubt, the sadness, etc. — beneath what they have said.

It's important to have thirty or forty minutes to work through this process with Impostors. Take the time to really listen and to let them know that you hear.

DON'T:

- Assume victims are helpless or unable to change.

- Withdraw from them because you can't seem to get them to hear your concern and your support.

- Give up after you've witnessed the Impostor Cycle several times. You may find yourself thinking, "She doesn't listen to me anyway. My reassurances never work." This reaction is only partly true.

- Be dishonest about how you feel.

DO:

- Let victims know by your words and actions that you love them and that you're not rejecting them.

- Help them feel temporarily better after going through the Impostor Cycle by showing this love. Although the victims don't change their basic profiles as a result of your love, it does help ease some of the pain. Your reassurance is very important and may help them not to panic.

- Be honest about your frustrations. Say, "I feel angry and sad when I can't seem to help," if this is the way you feel.

BEING SPECIFIC WITH PRAISE

In efforts to reassure others of our love and respect, it's

very easy to generalize how we feel. Such statements as, "You're wonderful," seem to pop out of our mouths. And although we honestly may believe that the person is wonderful, such generalized statements do not go very far in convincing IP sufferers that they are. Most have difficulty hearing any positive feedback, but they're more likely to hear it and believe it if the praise is specific. Therefore, the following guidelines may assist you as you continue to offer support.

DON'T:

- Make generalized statements when you give praise, such as, "You're great," "You're fantastic," "You know you're wonderful," or "Everyone loves you."

- Make generalized comments when trying to reassure them that they will do well on a particular project. For example, don't say, "You shouldn't be worried about giving this speech, because you know you always do well."

- Be dishonest or inaccurate in your praise. Although your efforts to assure the Impostor of your love may be sincere, they will soon pick up on the insincerity of your praise and doubt your love and their worth even more.

DO:

- Be specific when you give praise. Instead of giving the above kinds of generalized praise, think about the things the victim does well or the things you admire most about him or her, and give examples of those things in your praise. For example, say, "I'm impressed with your knowledge of and use of language."

"I love your looks, your energy, your curiosity."
"Others care about you because you're understanding and giving and because they admire your ability to put them at ease."

- Be specific when trying to reassure Impostors that they will do well on particular projects. For example, if the person is worried about giving a speech, say something such as, "You are able to get and keep an audience's attention. You have a good presence and a good speaking voice."

- Be honest, and give only praise that you believe.

WORST CASE SCENARIOS

Remember, IP victims have trouble hearing and believing even the most positive feedback, and they generally believe that no one understands how they feel. It's therefore important to show them that you're listening and paying attention to what they say and that you're trying to understand. When they begin to express their fears, the following DOs and DON'Ts will be helpful in letting you know how to respond.

DON'T:

- Immediately say that a catastrophe will not occur when they begin expressing the fear that they will fail.

DO:

- Ask how likely it is that a catastrophe will occur. For example, if the person is worried that he or she will fail an exam, ask the question, "How likely is it that this will happen?"

- Listen to the answers. If they say that it's very likely, then ask, "How many times have you failed such a test before?"

- Listen again. If they say that they've never failed before, tell them you believe that because: 1. They're good at taking tests; 2. They're well prepared; 3. They're experts on the subject; or, 4. Because their track record is so good, etc., you believe they probably will do well this time too.

- Ask, if they continue to believe that they will fail, what is the worst thing that could happen if they do.

ASSURING THAT YOUR LOVE IS NOT THE RESULT OF THEIR SUCCESS

In most cases, IP victims will respond that the worst thing that can happen is that they will lose your love. They probably believe that you care for them only because of their productivity or perfection. And if they fail at something, or appear less than perfect, they're afraid that you will think less of them and possibly want to abandon them.

Therefore, even if it's difficult or impossible for you to believe that the Impostor will fail at something, it's important for you to listen to their fears and assure them that you will love them even if they do.

DON'T:

- Say that you believe they could never fail. This will probably only make them worry all the more — since your expectations of them are so high — that if they do fail they will certainly lose your love. It probably will also make them think you aren't really listening and that you don't understand.

DO:

- Listen to their continued protests that they will fail.

- Let them know that you will love them and care for them if they indeed fail. (Again, remember to be honest and sincere. If you do not believe this — if you're afraid you wouldn't love the person if they weren't successful — then don't make such assurances.)

- Tell them that you love them for reasons other than their success. Again, be honest and be specific. If the person is afraid they will not get a promotion, say, "I don't love you because of where you are in the company. I love you because you're a kind and giving partner. I love you because of your sense of humor. I love your intelligence and your quick mind. And I will love you even if you don't get this promotion."

WHAT YOU'RE FEELING HAS A NAME

Most Impostors are relieved when they discover that

they're not alone. Their fears are often eased when they learn that other successful people are suffering in much the same way, that there is a term — "The Impostor Phenomenon" — for what they're experiencing, and that there is a possibility that you, their friend or lover, could understand.

DO:

- Help IP sufferers identify what is happening to them. Assure them that they are not alone in their suffering or in their beliefs that they can't continue doing well. Tell them that many successful people are haunted by the same kinds of fears.

- Let them know that you've been reading about the subject, and if they're interested, tell them what you've learned.

- Share information when it's relevant, and discuss specific aspects of their behavior (such as The Fear of Failure or The Need to Be Special, etc.).

- Ask if they think any of these things apply to them and if it's helpful to discuss them. Listen carefully to their answers.

DON'T:

- Overdo it and overwhelm them with all you've learned.

- Tell them things about the phenomenon if it makes them uncomfortable or if they imply it's information they don't want to hear.

DISCUSSING THE WELL-INTENTIONED MASK MAKERS

If the mood is good and the IP victims are receptive to hearing more about the phenomenon, you may want to discuss some of the family messages they may have received about success. You might want to go back to Chapter Four and have them answer the questions dealing with family dynamics. If this goes well, you might compare notes about your answers and theirs and swap family stories.

DON'T:

- Hold your family up as being better than theirs.

- Come across as being critical of their families. If you find it almost impossible not to be critical, then these conversations probably will not be productive. Or, you may need to be honest and say directly, "As we're talking about this, I'm finding myself being critical of your family because of what happened to you." When you admit how you feel, the victims may respond that they can't discuss their families with you. Or, there is the possibility that your feelings will give them some relief and actually help them not to be so guilty about how they feel.

Since you are not as immersed in their family system as the IP victims, you may be helpful in discovering some of the messages they have been receiving from their parents and siblings. If you can be observant without being overly critical, and if you two have begun to discuss the Impostor's family dynamics constructively and with ease, you may be able to point out certain patterns. For example, you might say, "Did you notice that your mother never mentioned your new job?" Or you might try to get the Impostor to start discussing things by carefully phrasing a question, such as, "How did you react when your father kept praising Bob and ignoring you?" By using such careful, caring approaches, you may be able to help IP victims understand some of the origins of their fears.

DON'T:

- Give advice, as you begin such discussions about the Impostor's family, unless you are directly asked for advice.

- Don't offer interpretations and suggestions.

DO:

- Listen when IP victims begin to become aware of how their family's messages are affecting them. Listen, listen, listen, and try to really hear and understand what they are saying.

- Be willing to support the victims when they experience sadness, fear, and anger as they recognize more about themselves and their families.

YOUR HELP MAY NOT BE ENOUGH

It's important for you to remember that, as much as you may care and as much as you may be willing to encourage, nurture, and patiently try to help, your help may not be enough. You and the Impostor together may begin to realize, especially after you've tried to discuss some of their feelings and looked more closely at their family dynamics, that professional help is needed. If this becomes the case,

DON'T:

• Think that you have failed or begin to blame yourself.

• Lose patience and say, "Why won't you listen to what I've been telling you? Why won't you believe this book?"

DO:

• Support and encourage the victims to get counseling or psychotherapy if they need it in order to cope with their fears or to change.

• Be willing to attend joint sessions if the counselor or psychotherapist believes it will be helpful.

• Recognize that with much practice and help, the person can learn to enjoy his or her successes.

WORKING FOR MORE JOY AND LESS WORK

Often, as much as they appear the opposite, Impostors

really want to have more joy in their lives, and they want to be less demanding of themselves and be less consumed by work. But because of many of their characteristics, these people may have trouble letting go and learning to be joyful.

If this is the case with your partner, try to find ways to entice him or her to have more joy and pure pleasure. Invite them to join you in activities that you both enjoy. And if you're the kind of person who is also overworked and possibly not relaxing enough, see if you can't find more ways for both of you to participate in fun activities that in no way involve conscious self-improvement. For example, for some people jogging or running is a real pleasure and a real release from professional demands and worries. But for others it's more like work and a form of self-improvement. For this second group of people, jogging would only add to the demands in their already busy lives, and another form of activity, such as tennis or reading or singing in a choir, would be more helpful.

DON'T:

- Spend lots of time criticizing IP victims for overworking or nagging them about their tendency to be so dedicated. Your nagging will not help.

DO:

- Try to find activities both of you can participate in that will bring more relaxation and enjoyment to your lives.

- Participate in endeavors that do not involve self-improvement, even if your Impostor partner will not join you. As you balance your own life with more pleasure-seeking time, you probably will serve as an inspiration to the IP sufferer.

Remember, IP victims generally are very sensitive, loving partners or friends who want to be loved and respected by those people they care about, and they usually work very hard at having good relationships. Let these people know specifically what you appreciate about your association with them. If you do so, and they learn to deal with their IP feelings, your relationship with them probably will become even richer.

Remember, too, that you may not be able to convince them yourself of how intelligent and talented and deserving they are. It may take professional counseling or psychotherapy work to help overcome intense Impostor fears.

Beverly and Michael, the young couple we discussed in Chapter Eleven, are a good example of such a case. Although Michael was patient and loving and tried as hard as he knew how to convince Beverly that she was a talented artist, his efforts did little good. He therefore became frustrated, angry, and sometimes felt as if maybe Beverly's self-doubt had something to do with him. Fortunately, he was willing to join her in several sessions of our therapy work, and as he changed the way he responded to her, she also began to change.

The next time Beverly began to doubt herself before the opening of one of her shows, instead of saying that her work was wonderful and that she shouldn't be nervous because she always did well, Michael responded in the following way:

"I can see that you're really anxious about this show."

"Yes, you know I am," Beverly snapped. "I'm scared to death."

"Why are you so scared?"

"Because I'm afraid the show will be a flop and that I'll get terrible reviews. I'm afraid no one will buy anything."

"Has that ever happened before?"

"What do you mean?"

"I mean have you ever had a show that was a flop before?"

"Well, no."

"Have you ever gotten terrible reviews?"

"No."

"Have you ever had a show where most of the paintings didn't sell?"

"No! All right, I get your point."

"I was just trying to determine," Michael said gently, "what the chances are of your having a real flop. What do you think the chances are?"

"I don't know," Beverly said. "I guess they're slim. But I'm still scared."

"I hear you, Bev. I really do. I know you're scared. But I also know you're a fine artist, and that your chances of failing are pretty small."

"But I might," she kept on.

"Yes, you might. And if you did, what's the worst thing that could happen to you?"

"Well . . . I don't know. I guess I'm afraid the other artists in town would laugh at me. Or that our friends would no longer like me."

"Do you think we have those kinds of friends?"

"No. No, of course I don't, but . . ."

"What about the artists? Do you think they would really laugh at you?"

"Some of them are pretty jealous."

"So they might?"

"Yeah, they might."

"Well, if they did, could you live with that? Could you pick up and keep going?"

"I don't know. I guess I could. Especially if you were here, and our friends supported me."

"Well, I'm always going to be here. I think you're a fantastic artist — creative, unique, willing to try new things — but I also love you for more reasons than that. I didn't marry you just because you paint beautiful pictures. I love you because you're the most caring person I've ever known. I love you because you have a great sense of humor, and because you make my life fulfilled and good. And I'd want to be married to you even if you never sold another canvas in your life. The only thing that would bother me is if you really stopped trying."

Beverly had very intense Impostor feelings, and she was not an easy person to convince. But because Michael was empathetic, patient, and encouraged her to get help, she slowly began to take off her Impostor Mask. And because of these kinds of responses to her IP doubts — where he showed her that he was listening to her fears and gave her specific examples of the things about her he admired — she began to be less afraid of failing.

The next time she had a one-woman show, she did succeed. And this time, because the two of them had worked together so well on discussing her fears and her doubts, she was better able to appreciate her success. That night after the opening, for the first time that Michael could remember, they were able to go to their favorite restaurant and genuinely, joyfully celebrate.

THE IMPOSTOR PHENOMENON

RAISING IMPOSTOR-FREE CHILDREN

Since changing IP feelings is often a long, difficult process, and since most of the characteristics are formed when the individual is a child, it seems obvious that we would want to prevent the Impostor Phenomenon from occurring among our children. Unfortunately, our society is more adept at dealing with cure than it is with prevention, and at present we know more about the origins of IP feelings than we do about preventing them.

The whole issue of effective parenting is also a very complex one, and there is considerable disagreement about the subject among child development experts, child psychologists, and parents. I will not attempt to deal with the entire issue, of course, but I will be offering some guidelines that have come out of my work in child guidance clinics and suggestions that have emerged as a result of studying the childhood backgrounds of many IP victims and their families. Although I believe these suggestions definitely can help, whether or not they absolutely prevent the phenomenon will not be determined until many parents, teachers, and child care specialists have tried them over a lengthy period of time.

GIVING THE CORRECT MESSAGES

As I have stated in several chapters of this book and indicated through various case histories, the kinds of messages — both verbal and nonverbal — that parents and siblings give to a child are extremely significant. From his or her family, the child receives cues about how to act in the world. And what the family says and does shapes how the child views himself and how he views the world.

When we studied the Impostor profile, one definite characteristic was the tendency to say, "I must be perfect . . ." or "I must be the very best. . ." or "I must be special, or I won't be loved." Somehow IP victims received the message that they would lose the love of their families if they were not outstanding performers; they did not believe they could be loved for themselves. These beliefs seemed most prevalent in cases where the victims had families that tended to be very critical of mistakes; where parents did not want to hear about problems or listen to their children's fears; and where parents were constantly conveying the message that their children should be the very best.

The most important element in the prevention of this aspect of the phenomenon is to communicate to children that they are loved, and that they are loved not because they bring home good grades or awards or perform particularly well, but because of themselves. Many parents falsely assume that their children know they are loved. But children do not take such a thing for granted, and they generally will not know it unless that love is communicated in words, smiles, hugs, warmth, and the parents' willingness to listen.

Talking with children, not *at* them, is essential here. Nationally known family therapist and author of *Conjoint Family Therapy*, Virginia Satir, suggests that parents need to kneel down occasionally so that they're at eye level with their children. She accurately observes that our children are seeing only our knees or our legs and rarely our faces. But if we get on their level, our chances of both hearing and being heard are far greater. If we look our children in the eyes, we're more apt to see how they feel and more likely to begin to honestly listen; and if they can look at our faces, they're more apt to open up about all the things they feel.

MASKING FEELINGS AND NEEDS: THE
FIRST STEP IN CREATING IMPOSTOR MASKS

It's often difficult for parents to communicate love for their children unless they're getting a certain amount of love and tenderness in their own lives. It's therefore important for parents not to hide these needs, but to admit them and try to satisfy them. If such needs cannot be met by a spouse or partner, then friends, networks, or support groups can be helpful — and in some cases critical — in preventing a kind of burnout in exhausted, overworked, and sometimes lonely adults.

Also, parents need to remember that it is almost impossible to be all-loving and all-caring all of the time. The feelings we have about our children are complex and often mixed. Of course we love them, but at times we become frustrated, angry, resentful, and occasionally feel that we are close to hating them, too. That's why support groups and talking with other parents are so important. If parents feel they're the only ones who have such mixed emotions, they're apt to feel guilty or possibly even crazy, and these feelings only harm the relationship with their children.

It's also important for parents to learn ways to be honest about these feelings with their children. If your child makes you angry, don't try to mask the anger; if you do, he or she probably will pick up on the tension and feel that there's something worse than anger going on in your head. Instead of hiding what you feel, say, "I dislike it when you do this," and explain why. Then tell the child the kind of behavior you expect. Through such honest communication, children learn that parents can be as frustrated, angry, tired, and imperfect as anyone else. Knowing such things takes some of the pressure off children, and they learn that it's OK for them to express such emotions, too.

It is a cliché, I know, to say that you must first love and respect yourself before others will do the same. But in the case of our children, I think this is a critical point and one that needs repeating. If you have suffered IP feelings and still believe that you have to be perfect in order to be loved, your children will sense this and probably apply it to themselves. But if you can be honest about how you feel and admit that you are often imperfect and that you have needs, your chances of communicating with your children are much greater. It also helps them know that you're authentically showing them how you feel; and if you're authentic about your anger, they'll be able to know that you're also authentic about your love.

LISTENING TO DOUBTS AND FEARS

When children express doubts about their talents, intelligence, looks, or other qualities they believe are important, it's easy for caring parents to respond in a generalized way. For example, if Jennifer spills her glass of iced tea and chastises herself by saying, "I'm so dumb," it's easy to say, "Of course you're not dumb. You're brilliant, Jennifer. You can do anything." But chances are that if you reply this way, Jennifer will begin to believe that you aren't really listening to her. She thinks to herself, "Mom thinks I can do anything. She doesn't know how stupid I sometimes feel."

But if you take the time to explain to Jennifer that everyone, even you, makes mistakes, then she begins to feel that maybe it's all right for her to occasionally mess up, too. And if you go a step further and explain that errors don't make someone stupid, but that, in fact, they sometimes help people to learn more quickly or more thoroughly, then Jennifer will begin to understand that you are listening to her, that you're sympathetic of her fears, and that you don't expect her to be perfect all of the time.

If Jennifer continues to be critical of herself, ask her why she thinks she's dumb. Sit down with her and really listen to what she's saying. As she begins to let you in on her frustrations, doubts, and fears, let her know that these things are being heard. Tell her that you sometimes have similar worries, too. Then begin giving her specific kinds of encouragement and praise. If she's a good artist, tell her you think so; next begin pointing out exactly why you think she's a good artist — the way she applies colors, the feel she has for composition, the way she's able to paint landscapes so well. Again, be specific, and let her know that there are many lovable things about her and that she has talents you admire.

TEACHING SKILLS

Many of my clients who suffer from the Impostor Phenomenon grew up comparing themselves to their parents, and as adults they feel more than ever like Impostors because their parents were so much more competent than they. As we talk, I learn that the parents of these victims often were impatient individuals who made high demands of their children but were not willing to slowly and patiently teach them skills.

One young woman I saw said that her mother could do anything — manage a career, cook, sew, run a large house, and entertain. "I can't do any of those things," the woman complained.

"You have a good career, don't you?" I asked.

"Yes. But that's it. I'm a disaster in the kitchen. I can't

sew. I don't know the first thing about running a house, and whenever I even think of having to give a party, I panic. I tell you, I can't do any of those things."

During further discussions, I found out that this woman's mother only rarely had tried to teach her daughter any of these things, and when she did, it was a fiasco. She had no patience with her daughter, and if she didn't learn something within the first ten or fifteen minutes, the woman immediately quit trying.

"No wonder you don't know how to do any of those things," I said. "Most of those skills come with time, and you usually can't learn them by yourself."

"My mother did."

"Did she?" I asked.

As it turned out, the woman had grown up in a household not only with her own mother, but with a grandmother and an aunt. These three women had taught her all the skills that she seemed to possess so easily. When the daughter realized this, she was relieved and began to understand why she felt so incompetent.

Having patience and teaching skills can sometimes be difficult, especially if your life is extremely hectic and filled. Therefore, you may not be able to do all the teaching yourself. But you can encourage your children and let them know how much you enjoy their learning by providing opportunities for them to learn from grandparents, aunts, cousins, neighbors, etc. There are also many classes, workshops, and programs that can provide great learning environments for your child. And if you convey the message that you think it's important and enjoyable to learn, they'll begin to think the same thing. The important thing is for children to be able to find skills they feel competent in and interests that are specifically theirs.

As they begin learning these skills, overtly acknowledge and recognize their success. One way of doing this is to ask what they've learned in school, and then tell them you're pleased at their progress in particular areas. If a child is bright and always does well in school, don't fall into the trap of taking him or her for granted or bragging about them only to others. And when a child says that something is difficult for him, acknowledge that you understand and discuss the problems he's having. For example, if little Helen tells you she's worried about her math test or keeps claiming that she's "so stupid" about numbers, don't dismiss her concern by saying, "You're not stupid at anything. You'll do fine on the test." Instead, ask why she's afraid or why she thinks she's stupid, and then listen to what she says.

BEING HONEST

If a child begins behaving in a way that you don't like, instead of masking what you think and labeling the child — "You're lazy." "You're selfish." "You're spoiled." — let the child know you're not pleased. It's much better to talk about a behavior or action rather than to tell the child what kind of person he is (lazy, selfish, spoiled, etc.) and not really let him know specifically what has made you angry or what you dislike.

If you find yourself being highly critical of a child — either overtly by your actions and words, or covertly by mentally being aware of how he could be better — then it's important to get some help in understanding why you are this way. Possibly something is being touched off in you that is unfinished from your own childhood. But whatever the reason, it's important to remember that critical, demanding parents evoke IP feelings in their children.

FINDING TIME FOR PLAY

The last thing I would like to suggest is that you find time to play with your children. IP victims are the kinds of people who most often know more about work than about having fun, and they tend to come from families where little time was spent in play. It's therefore important to show children that you can work hard but that you still need time to relax and enjoy all the benefits your hard work brings.

Even if it's difficult to do so, try to find this special time with your children. If you have less tension, less stress, and less anger in your life, so will your children.

So many modern parents are willing to read, learn, listen, and be open with their children that I hope there soon will be a decrease in the number of people who suffer from the Impostor Phenomenon. So many elements help to create IP feelings that it's difficult to say exactly what will and what will not cause them. But if I had to give a bottom-line statement about how such unproductive feelings and characteristics are formed, it would be this — parents who mask their thoughts, their praise, their love, their tenderness, and their own fears and self-doubts are most likely to put an Impostor Mask on the faces of their children.

16 | Suggested Reading

IN THE FIRST half of this chapter, you will find a list of books and articles that may assist you in understanding the Impostor Phenomenon and its causes, prevention, and treatment. Although this is not an exhaustive self-help list, the material recommended here can provide you with an in-depth look at some of the issues related to IP feelings.

There is also a list in the last half of the chapter which contains articles and books for researchers of the phenomenon and for professional counselors or therapists who may want to read the original articles on the treatment issues of the Impostor Phenomenon.

I

Burns, David. *Feeling Good: The New Mood Therapy.* Signet. New York. 1981.
A very good book that explains cognitive therapy, an approach that can be helpful to IP victims as they work to change the Impostor Cycle.
Buscaglia, Leo. *Living, Loving and Learning.* Ballantine Books. New York. 1982.
A wonderful book about life, love, and learning. His

chapter on children is superb. Buscaglia teaches about
zest and joy in living and learning, and he challenges
people to take risks and to dare to experiment. This
book can provide real inspiration for Impostors,
especially those who have had difficulty changing and
taking risks.

Clance, P. R. and Imes, S. "The Impostor Phenomenon in
High-Achieving Women: Dynamics and Therapeutic
Intervention." *Psychotherapy: Theory, Research and
Practice.* 1978, 15. 241-247.

The original article in which Dr. Imes and I coined the
term and explained the dynamics involved. We also discussed the causes of the Impostor Phenomenon and
recommended treatment strategies. We received hun-
dreds of requests for the article because so many people
were relieved to finally have some written information
about what they were experiencing.

Dreikurs, Rudolph and Grey, Loren. *Logical Consequences.* Merideth Press. New York. 1968.

An excellent book on discipline which develops the
concept that children learn best when they experience
the logical consequences of their behaviors. A productive way to deal with discipline and relevant to the
prevention of IP feelings in children.

Ellis, Albert and Knaus, William J. *Overcoming Procrastination.* Signet. New York. 1979.

Some IP sufferers, out of their terror of failure and their
fear that they won't be the very best, begin to procrastinate. This book highlights the attitudes that lead to this
characteristic.

Freudenberger, Herbert J. with Richelson, Geraldine.
Burnout. Bantam. New York. 1981.

Dr. Freudenberger helps readers identify what burnout

is and provides a test to help you determine if you're suffering from it. The book gives very good suggestions on how to beat the high cost of success.

Friedman, Martha. *Overcoming the Fear of Success*. Seaview Books. New York. 1980.

An in-depth analysis of the titled subject and ways to cope with it. I highly recommend this book for IP victims who have a real fear of success.

Ginott, Haim G. *Between Parent and Child*. Avon Books. New York. 1965.

A very good book on parenting with fundamental principles that are excellent and particularly relevant in the prevention of IP feelings in children.

Machlowitz, Marilyn. *Workaholics: Living with Them, Working with Them*. Mentor. New York. 1981.

This book provides understanding and help for those IP victims who tend to overprepare and overwork and for those people who love them and work with them.

Olds, Sally Wendkos. *The Working Parent's Survival Guide*. Bantam. New York. 1983.

A very fine resource book for parents. Very practical information to help you with your children, your job, your marriage. There are many suggestions here on how to save time and when to get help.

Pleck, Joseph and Sawyer, Jack. *Men and Masculinity*. Prentice Hall. New York. 1974.

A fine book that discusses the kinds of changes that men are facing in the twentieth century. It looks at the messages men have received about masculinity, messages that are often relevant to male IP victims who deal with fear of failure and fear of success.

Rapoport, Rhona and Rapoport, Robert N. with Janice Bumstead. *Working Couples*. Harper and Row. New

York. 1978.

A book that discusses the issues and solutions of couples who both have paying jobs. Deals with very practical matters such as choosing child care, finding employment, parenting, and work sharing.

Ruddick, Sara and Daniels, Pamela, editors. *Working it Out.* Pantheon Books. New York. 1977.

In this book twenty-three women writers, artists, scientists, and scholars talk about their lives and their careers and how they work it all out. A powerful book in which women discuss the problems, challenges, obstacles, and joys in doing what they want to do with their lives. Indirectly touches on many of the IP feelings.

Shaevitz, Marjorie Hansen. *The Superwoman Syndrome.* Warner Books. New York. 1984.

An excellent resource book for women who expect themselves to be perfect in every aspect of their lives. Very pertinent to IP victims who have such high expectations for themselves.

Steiner, Claude. *Scripts People Live: Transactional Analysis of Life Scripts.* Grove Press. New York. 1974.

A superb book that deals with the important messages people receive from their families. IP victims often obtain life scripts about their intelligence, success, and failure. This is therefore an excellent source book that gives an in-depth understanding of how these scripts are made and what can be done to change them.

II

Flewelling, Ann. (1985). *The impostor phenomenon in individuals succeeding in self-perceived atypical professions; The effects of mentoring. A Thesis.* Georgia State

University, Atlanta, Georgia.

Gibbs, Margaret S. (1984). "The therapist as impostor." In Claire Brody (ed.), *Women therapists working with women.* Springer Publishing Company, Inc. New York. 1984.

Grays, Linda. (1985). *The relation between the impostor phenomenon and atypicality of race, educational attainment, socio-economic status and career in college women. A Thesis.* Georgia State University, Atlanta, Georgia.

Harvey, J.C. (1981). *The impostor phenomenon and achievement: A failure to internalize success* (Doctoral dissertation, Temple University, 1981). *Dissertation Abstracts International,* 42, 4969B.

Hirschfeld, M.M. (1982). *The impostor phenomenon in successful career women* (Doctoral dissertation, Fordham University, 1982). *Dissertation Abstracts International,* 43, 1722A.

Imes, S.A. (1979). *The impostor phenomenon as a function of attribution patterns and internalized femininity/masculinity in high-achieving women and men.* (Doctoral dissertation, Georgia State University, 1979). *Dissertation Abstracts International,* 40, 5868B-5869B.

Imes, Suzanne and Clance, Pauline Rose. "Treatment of the impostor phenomenon in high-achieving women." In Claire Brody (ed.), *Women therapists working with women.* Springer Publishing Company, Inc. New York. 1984.

Lawler, N.K. (1984). *The impostor phenomenon in high-achieving persons and Jungian personality variables.* (Doctoral dissertation, Georgia State University, 1984). *Dissertation Abstracts International,* 45, 86.

Matthews, Gail and Clance, Pauline Rose. "Treatment of

the impostor phenomenon in psychotherapy clients." *Psychotherapy in Private Practice.* January, 1985.

Stahl, J. M., Turner, H. M., Wheeler, A. E., and Elbert, P. (1980). *The "impostor phenomenon" in high school and college science majors.* Paper presented at the meeting of the American Psychological Association, Montreal.

Topping, M. E. H. (1983). *The impostor phenomenon: A study of its construct and incidence in university faculty members.* (Doctoral dissertation, University of South Florida, 1983). *Dissertation Abstracts International,* 44, 1948B-1949B.

Trotman, Frances K. "Psychotherapy of black women and the dual effects of racism and sexism." In Claire Brody (ed.), *Women therapists working with women.* Springer Publishing Company, Inc. New York. 1984.